Discovering
W🌎RLD GEOGRAPHY
with Books Kids Love

Nancy A. Chicola and Eleanor B. English

fulcrum resources

Golden, Colorado

Library of Congress Cataloging-in-Publication Data

Chicola, Nancy A.
    Discovering world geography with books kids love / Nancy A. Chicola and Eleanor B. English.
        p.   cm.
    Includes bibliographical references and index.
    ISBN 1-55591-965-0 (pbk.)
    1. Geography—Study and teaching (Elementary)—Methodology. 2. Geography—Study and teaching (Secondary)—Methodology. 3. Children's literature. I. English, Eleanor B. II. Title.
G73.C513   1999
910'.71—dc21   98-49150
                                                                                                                              CIP

Printed in the United States of America
0 9 8 7 6 5 4 3 2 1

Book and cover design: Bill Spahr
Interior photographs: Richard Gates
Interior art: Theresa Heinz
Maps were produced by Fulcrum Publishing using Cartesia MapArt™
and the Rand McNally *Portrait World Atlas* as guides.

Fulcrum Publishing
350 Indiana Street, Suite 350
Golden, Colorado 80401-5093
(800) 992-2908 • (303) 277-1623
www.fulcrum-resources.com

Contents

Acknowledgments

Any venture takes not only planning and direction but assistance from people who aid the process by freely giving of their time and expertise. To these individuals we express our appreciation:

Saint Bonaventure University's Friedsam Library staff, Ann Tenglund and Martha Drake, and a special acknowledgment to Theresa Shaffer for her timely acquisition of books on interlibrary loan.

Elizabeth Ormiston, Alisa Smith, and Gwendolyn Agthe, graduate assistants, who made many trips to the library to search for books and check sources.

Students in social studies methods classes who proved to be our laboratory in the activities for the literature-geography connection.

Donna Ward and the students at Boardmanville Elementary School and Beverly Ingle and her sixth-grade students at Laredo Middle School who participated in some of the activities and served as models for the photographs.

Colleagues Dr. Richard Gates for his photographic expertise and Theresa Heinz, who took our activities and created the artistic images that so effectively illustrate this book.

Sam Sheldon for his geographic expertise and materials and willingness to answer questions concerning the finer points of geography.

Michael Chicola for his patience and support during the many hours of geographic discussion that disrupted his weekends.

Susan, Pamela, Joseph, and Michelle English for their steadfast support and encouragement.

Suzanne Barchers, our editorial cartographer, who charted the sometimes murky and often complex journey in mapping the path to the successful completion of this book.

Introduction

Geography is the fundamental focal point for studying the earth and people upon it. Geography plays a role in everyone's life, yet there has been considerable concern about the lack of geographical knowledge, skills, and perspectives among young learners. Schools continually attempt to raise standards for students, but many students fail to achieve even a basic level of geographic knowledge. The study of geography is an integrative process, not merely the study of isolated geographic facts, as it has been taught traditionally. What is needed is a new perspective that involves and interests students, teachers, and parents as well.

Teaching geography using children's literature is an approach that aids geographical understanding. The interaction among people, places, and environments can be illuminated through children's literature. Fiction and nonfiction books have always played a role in children's lives, both in school and at home; they have been used to both inform and entertain. Trade books of various genres can play important roles as motivating maps for young geographers.

Discovering World Geography with Books Kids Love focuses on an audience of primary (K–2), bridge (2–4), and intermediate (4–6) students and can be used easily by both teachers and parents. To clarify the geographical concepts in fiction and nonfiction literature, trade books of each type are used. Picture storybooks, folktales, legends, myths, wordless books, and chapter books populate the selected fiction titles. Concept, alphabet, and information books, including biographies and chapter books, constitute the nonfiction trade titles. In both types, a variety of books, old and more recent, appropriate for the selected ages and interests of the students, are included. Not only are these books examples of quality children's literature, but the content is apropos to the substance of geography as well.

Nonfiction books provide physical and cultural geographic information. *The Remarkable Voyages of Captain Cook* by Rhoda Blumberg, for example, brings to light the Pacific Realm as it was sailed, explored, and recorded by James Cook, the navigator, and Joseph Banks, the botanist. One aspect of the fauna of North America is the birds that migrate to certain regions. Using *The Birds of Summer* by Carol Lerner as a reference, adults and children have an opportunity to identify, observe, and maintain habitats for these seasonal visitors.

Fictional trade books are primarily geared toward entertaining the student. In this genre, the geographical information is inherent rather than explicit in the text. We have created activities based on the locations, settings, characters, and plots of stories that will increase geographical understanding and skill, such as we do for *The Magic Fan* by Keith Baker. In the story, the *tsunami,* the tidal wave preceded by earthquakes that is typical of Japan, is interwoven into the story. As supplements to this book, we present readers with activities that provide them with in-depth experiences of this phenomenon. For grades K–2, generally the pictures rather than the limited text of the trade books provide the foundation for mapping activities. We have reviewed the content of the books and developed activities that align with the interrelated themes of geography outlined by the Committee on Geographic Education in the *Guidelines for Geographic Education: Elementary and Secondary Schools* and the Essential Elements and National Geography Standards published in *Geography for Life—National Geography Standards (1994)* (see Appendix).

Throughout the centuries geographers have held different opinions as to how the world should be mapped. Continents, regions, and realms are but three ways. H. J. de Blij and Peter Muller presented the world divided into twelve geographic realms: Europe, Russia, North America, Middle America, South America, North Africa/Southwest Asia, Subsaharan Africa, South Asia, East Asia, Southeast Asia, Australia, and the Pacific.[1] The broad global framework of realms consists of spatial units composed of lands or countries based on their physical and cultural factors. We chose the realm structure as the mapping framework because it appears to be the most appropriate for promoting geographic learning. The geographic realms serve as chapter titles throughout the book. Trade books have been selected that highlight the geographic knowledge, skills, and perspectives relevant to each of the realms. The number of books used varies based on the size and uniqueness of each specific realm and the availability of quality trade books in print for that realm.

Two realms receive special focus. First, since Japan has recently been included in the East Asian Realm with China, we have expanded the activities and literature because of Japan's cultural and traditional uniqueness and its position as an economic world power. Second, with the demise of the former Soviet Union, former Western bloc countries are now categorized as East Europe within the European Realm. We have added books and activities to the European Realm to include the cultural diversity of these countries.

Each realm chapter is formatted into the following four sections, and a comprehensive glossary appears at the end of the book.

Getting Your Bearings

This section provides the reader with a map and a brief description of the location, regions, topography, climate, flora, fauna, and other unique features of the specific realm. It becomes a concise reference that helps set the physical and cultural milieu for the geographic experiences that follow.

Mapping

For a specific realm, the reader will find authors, titles, genres, appropriate grade levels (primary, K–2; bridge, 2–4; intermediate, 4–6), and relevant elements and themes for the selected books. A short synopsis of every book included within a realm section is given as well.

Statements of key geographic understandings based on each book integrate knowledge, skills, and perspectives into comprehensive conclusions that students can apply to the physical and cultural components of any realm. The knowledge segment is written in measurable terms and serves as the connection between the content information from the books and appropriate physical, cultural, and geographical subject matter for each realm. By using the five skills in geography linked to the knowledge sections, students will have the tools to ask questions; gather, organize, and analyze information; and answer questions. Two perspectives, spatial and ecological, are bonded with knowledge and skills and serve as geographic lenses to develop student attitudes, values, and beliefs.

Each activities section is structured for three modes of participation: I, Individual; P, Pairs; and G, Group. A framework of creative and basic activities provides a hands-on approach. The initiating activity for each book focuses on location and place and is preceded by a list of guiding questions. All of the activities fit the appropriate grade levels and stimulate interest as well as higher-order thinking. A list of essential materials requisite for implementation accompanies each activity. In addition, each realm includes reproducible art for use in the activities. The reproducible art is found at the end of this section.

When using a wall map for activities that involve outlining borders, cover the map with contact paper for durability. For individual maps for student use, use black-line masters provided by a textbook series or purchase masters at a teacher supply store.

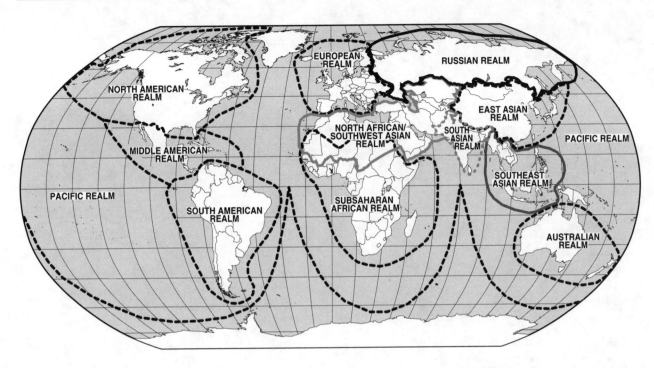

The above map shows the twelve geographic realms as discussed in this book. The representation of the boundaries varies (e.g., use of solid lines, use of dotted lines) to designate overlapping and adjacent realms.

Charting with More Books

We have selected other suitable books for each realm. Space limitations preclude the inclusion of key understandings, knowledge, skills, perspectives, and activities for all of these books. The genres, levels, elements, themes, and a brief description of each book are provided so that teachers and parents may create relevant activities to further promote geographic learning about the realms.

Realm References

At the conclusion of each realm, we provide bibliographic information on the books used for Mapping and Charting.

Glossary

Definitions of geographical terms and processes mentioned in or supplementary to the realms appear at the end of the book.

With books kids love, students, teachers, and parents are ready to embark on this exciting journey of mapping the world. *Bon voyage!*

[1] de Blij, H. J., and P. Muller. 1997. *Geography: Realms, Regions, and Concepts*, 8th ed. New York: John Wiley & Sons, pp. 2–5.

Chapter 1
European Realm

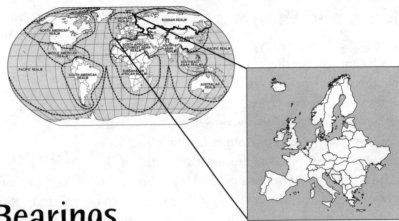

Getting Your Bearings

Location

Europe, as a realm, includes western and eastern European countries, with the exception of Russia, a realm in itself. Spanning 2,191,243 square miles, Europe is bordered on the west by the Atlantic Ocean, on the east by Russia, on the north by the Arctic Ocean, and on the south by the Mediterranean and Black Seas. Europe is located between 35°N and 71°N latitude and 24°W and 40°E longitude. This realm differs from others in the diversity of its people and the multitude of nations, thirty-eight, that it encompasses. Western Europe includes Great Britain, Ireland, Denmark, Norway, Sweden, Finland, Iceland, France, Belgium, Netherlands, Luxembourg, Germany, Switzerland, Austria, Liechtenstein, Spain, Portugal, Italy, Greece, and Malta. Eastern Europe consists of Poland, Czech Republic, Slovakia, Hungary, Romania, Bulgaria, Albania, Yugoslavia, Slovenia, Croatia, Bosnia and Herzegovina, Macedonia, Estonia, Latvia, Lithuania, Belarus, Moldova, and Ukraine. The five most populous cities, all located in western Europe, are, in descending order, Paris, London, Milan, Madrid, and Athens.

Topography

Four major physiographic regions comprise Europe: Central Uplands, North European Lowlands, Western Uplands, and Alpine Mountains. Within the Central Uplands lie low mountains and high plateaus, including the Massif Central of France. The North European Lowlands encompasses flat and rolling land that includes fertile farmland and several major rivers, including the Rhine, Seine, Weser, Elbe, Vistula, Dnieper, and Danube. The Western Uplands, located on the western edge of Europe, contains Meseta in central Spain as well as the Scottish Highlands and the mountains of Scandinavia. The highest mountain ranges in Europe are within the Alpine Mountains: the Pyrenees, the Alps, the Sierra Nevada, the Apennines, and the Dinaric and Carpathian Ranges. Mont Blanc in the Alps, 15,771 feet above sea level, is the highest point.

Europe has an irregular coastline, including many small and large islands, such as Ireland and the British Isles, and peninsulas, such as the Scandinavian, Iberian, Apennine, and Balkan. The world's largest saltwater lake, the Caspian Sea, lies within this realm.

Climate

The climate ranges from Mediterranean in the south to alpine in the highest and far north regions. Most of Europe has a temperate four-season climate. January temperatures average from -4° to 14°F around the Arctic Circle to over 50°F in the southern areas of Spain, Italy, and Greece. In July temperatures in Reykjavík, Iceland, average 48°F, while in London, Paris, and Berlin they average 64°F. The hottest July temperatures occur in Madrid and Palermo at an average of 77°F. The temperatures in many areas are moderated by coastal locations. Coastal and mountain areas average the heaviest rainfall, ranging from 40 to over 80 inches annually. The vast expanse of interior Europe averages 20 to 40 inches, with the exception of 10 to 20 inches in Ukraine, in central Spain, and above the Arctic Circle.

Flora and Fauna

Plants grow in three types of areas: forests, grasslands, and tundra/high mountains. The forests in northern Europe consist primarily of evergreens, while those in the central and southern areas are either broadleaf or mixed evergreens and broadleafs. Cork and olive trees are prominent along the Mediterranean coast. Grasses are most plentiful in the central and southern parts of the North European lowlands. Heather in Scotland, edelweiss in Austria and Switzerland, rockrose in Greece, and pasque-flower in Ukraine are common wildflowers. Lichens, mosses, and small shrubs are found in the tundra in the summer in Europe's Arctic and high mountain areas.

Northern Scandinavia is home to one of the largest bears, the European brown bear. The chamois and the ibex can be found in the high mountains of southwestern Europe, while elk and reindeer live in various parts of the realm from the Arctic to the Mediterranean. Some common birds include the stork, nightingale, puffin, egret, raven, and falcon. Because of Europe's great expanse of shoreline along the Atlantic Ocean and five major seas, the realm also has a variety of sea life, including seals, salmon, anchovy, herring, and sturgeon.

Unique Features

The heart of Western civilization began in Greece and Italy, though philosophy, science, art, and religion that grew from European beginnings spread through colonization to the Americas, Australia, and New Zealand. Language has played a role in the development of numerous separate cultures and political entities. The European realm contains a multiplicity of differences, yet the proximity of the nations fosters a common bond. Recently the formation of the European Union has strengthened that bond through an economic and political structure that many of the nations have joined.

Mapping

Pompeii ... Buried Alive!

Projection:	*Pompeii ... Buried Alive!* by Edith Kunhardt, 1987
Genre:	Information Book
Level:	Bridge (2–4)
Elements:	I. The World in Spatial Terms; II. Places and Regions; III. Physical Systems
Themes:	Location; Place; Region

The Book

Text and drawings graphically depict the story of Pompeii, the ancient Roman town nestled below the sleeping giant, Mount Vesuvius, today an ash-cinder volcano with a conical depression at the top. The book relates the life of the people of Pompeii during that fateful day nearly two thousand years ago when the mountain erupted. Deep inside, heated gases and rock created an explosion of hot ash and pebbles that hid the sun and spread over the town. For two days the eruption trapped people and animals, burying them alive.

A few people escaped by boat, including Pliny, the Roman naturalist who wrote about the event. His words were forgotten, as was Pompeii, for hundreds of years, until tunnel diggers chanced upon an old town wall. Archaeologists began digging carefully and unearthed the ancient Roman city that still lies beneath the now sleeping giant.

Key Understandings

The forces of nature change people's lives. A volcano is a force that can present a danger to the people who live in close proximity to it.

Knowledge

- Find the location of Pompeii and Mount Vesuvius.
- Describe the typical life of Pompeiians.
- Detail the forces at work in Mount Vesuvius that caused the eruption.
- Explain the consequences of the eruption of Mount Vesuvius.
- Compare and contrast the present state of Pompeii with the past.

Skills

- Ask questions about volcanoes and volcanic eruptions.
- Ask questions about Pompeii and its people.
- Gather information concerning Pompeii and volcanoes, Mount Vesuvius in particular.
- Analyze the Mount Vesuvius eruption.
- Create a model that accurately depicts the events of A.D. 79 in Pompeii.

Perspectives

Value the power that physical forces play in shaping the earth and human existence.

Activities

I = Individual   P = Pairs   G = Group

A. Visiting Vesuvius (I)

Materials: atlas, globe, wall map of Europe

Have the students locate Italy on the globe and wall map of Europe. In the atlas, discover the location of Pompeii and Mount Vesuvius. Identify any safe harbors nearby.

Questions to Ask

1. Where is Italy located relative to other countries in Europe?
2. Where in Italy did you find Pompeii? What is its absolute and its relative location?
3. What is the elevation of Mount Vesuvius? Is it the only volcano in Italy? If not, what are the others?
4. Based on Pompeii's location, what do you think life was like there in A.D. 79? What do you think life is like today?

B. Profiling Vesuvius (P)

Materials: several colors of modeling clay, pencils, scissors, cardboard square, *Dictionary of the Earth* by John Farndon, atlas or other geography sources

Using the drawing from page 7 of *Pompeii … Buried Alive!* and illustrations on page 53 of *Dictionary of the Earth* or another suitable source, on the cardboard square create a facsimile profile of an ash-cinder volcano out of modeling clay. Distinguish layers with different colors and label all parts of the cone. Use scissors and pencils to create dimensions of stone, rock, and magma on the clay. Display models.

A profile of the volcano.

c. Modeling Pompeii, Past and Present (G)

Materials: white index stock (70 wt.), crayons, paints, markers, white glue, transparent tape, scissors, two large cardboard boxes (e.g., refrigerator or stove), plastic human and animal figures

To establish a foundation for Pompeii, past and present, cut two large boxes so that a foundation and a frame (wall) are created from each. Set this aside and begin working in groups of four to five students on the structures in the community. Half of each group should focus on Pompeii past while the other half focuses on Pompeii present. In addition, each group should determine the structures for which it will be responsible. Teachers should coordinate the structure assignments so that a completed town will result. White index stock can be folded to form bases for buildings of various sizes, while roofs can be created by folding appropriately sized pieces of index stock in half and placing them on top. Before gluing or taping the structures, students should paint, color, and otherwise decorate according to the sources. One student from each group could have the task of decorating the walls around the outside of the large box. Place all structures and plastic figures in their respective boxes, making sure that past and present are mirror images as far as location is concerned.

Madeline's Rescue

Projection:	*Madeline's Rescue* by Ludwig Bemelmans, 1993
Genre:	Picture Storybook
Level:	Primary (K–2)
Elements:	I. The World in Spatial Terms; II. Places and Regions
Themes:	Location; Place; Region

The Book

Set in Paris, this rhyming story narrates another adventure of the impetuous Madeline. On a walk with Miss Clavel and her schoolmates, Madeline fell into the River Seine. She was rescued by a dog when others could not save her. The girls from the school adopted this homeless pooch, Genevieve, who participated in all of their activities from school work to daily walks. In May, the trustees came for their annual inspection and were aghast to see the new "student." Genevieve was ordered to leave and disappeared. Sadly, the girls and their teacher began a search through the streets of Paris. They returned home disappointed. During the night, Miss Clavel was awakened three times. The first was to discover Genevieve; the second to calm the girls' dispute over sleeping rights with the dog; and the third, most surprisingly and importantly, to welcome Genevieve's puppies. Now there was no more conflict, for each little girl had her own special dog.

Key Understandings

Cities around the world reflect distinctive styles that are based upon physical geography as well as the cultural patterns of those who inhabit them. Paris is one of the most important cities in Europe because of its history, architecture, and location on the Seine.

Knowledge

- Identify the location of Paris.
- Describe the importance of the Seine to the story.
- Identify and describe important landmarks in Paris, especially those that Madeline and her schoolmates see.
- Compare Paris landmarks to familiar local buildings and physical forms.

Skills

- Ask questions about the relative location of France.

- Ask questions about the Seine and the landmarks of Paris.
- Find information and pictures about Paris.
- Discuss the landmarks in the sequence of the scenes in the book.
- Analyze the landmarks according to type, size, and features.
- Answer questions concerning architecture and the River Seine.

Perspectives

Appreciate the beauty of human contribution to the landscape of Paris, such as architecture, park design, avenues, and bridges.

Activities

I = Individual   P = Pairs   G = Group

A. PINPOINTING PARIS (G)

Materials: primary globe, wall map of France, outline map of France, pencils, crayons, gummed stars

Using the globe, have students locate France and compare its size to the United States. On the wall map of France, have students trace with their hands the outline of the country and make a mental picture of it. Locate Paris and the River Seine on the wall map. Color the country in green on the outline map of France and label it. Find the River Seine and color it blue. Place a star on the Seine showing the location of Paris, and label it.

Questions to Ask

1. Where is France located on the globe? Where is the United States located?
2. How does the size of the United States compare to that of France?
3. What does the shape of France look like to you?
4. In what part of France is Paris located? What river flows through Paris? How do you know it is a river?

B. PARIS PROFILE (P)

Materials: simple outline map of Paris (reproducible), crayons, pencils, the book *Madeline's Rescue*, scissors, white glue

Using the reproducible map (see Figure 1.2 on page 8), landmarks, and the book, have students identify landmarks at each numbered point, using the Picture Key (see Figure 1.1 on page 7) as a guide. Glue pictures next to the numbered points on the map of Paris. Connect the points and retell Madeline's story using the outline map as a visual aid.

C. COMMUNITY COMPARISON (G)

Materials: instant cameras, film, paper, punch, glue, pencils, yarn or ribbon

Take a walk around the community to observe the landmarks and physical forms. Photograph places of interest to each group and compare to Madeline's locale. Have each group create a rescue storybook with the photographed landmarks inserted throughout. In consultation with the teacher, each group will determine how the final product will be published. Have groups share and display their storybooks.

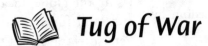 # Tug of War

Projection:	*Tug of War* by Joan Lingard, 1992
Genre:	Historical Fiction; Chapter Book
Level:	Intermediate (4–6)
Elements:	I. The World in Spatial Terms; II. Places and Regions; IV. Human Systems
Themes:	Location; Place; Region; Movement; Human/Environment Interaction

The Book

The time was September 1944. The location was Latvia, and the Russians were advancing through the country. Professor Lukas Petersons knew he must take his wife and children, Tomas and twins Hugo and Astra, to Germany or be captured and sent to Siberia. The family left home and began the journey that was to be full of danger, deprivation, and despair. The goal was Leipzig, where a professor friend would take in the family. When boarding a train, the surging crowd separated Hugo from the family. Astra and the family made the train just as it was leaving, assuming that Hugo would be following on the next train. Discovering that the professor in Leipzig was dead, the Petersons joined other refugees traveling westward to meet the U.S. army. Hugo's train went to Hamburg, where he was cared for by a German family. When well enough to travel, he went to Leipzig, discovered the professor's house in ashes, and believed his family was dead. Hugo returned to Hamburg to live permanently with the German family.

The Petersons lived in a Latvian refugee camp in Stuttgart for three years before the word came from Canada about a job and a home. Astra never stopped searching and asking others about her twin. Just before the Petersons were to leave Stuttgart, Astra visited Hamburg, where she saw a young blond man with eyeglasses. It was Hugo. To their joy, the twins and the family were reunited.

Key Understandings

Often, when another nation forcibly dominates lands and peoples, the will to survive and the search for freedom become the driving forces. The Latvian people suffered greatly at the hands of the Russian invaders, yet many managed to reach freedom by journeying to other lands.

Knowledge

- Identify the location of Latvia.
- Describe the route between Latvia and Leipzig that was followed by the Petersons.
- Compare and contrast the cities of Hamburg, Leipzig, and Stuttgart in 1945 with those same cities today.
- Determine the impact of physical, political, and cultural geography as causes and effects of conflict.

Skills

- Ask questions concerning the routes of Hugo and Astra in their search for freedom.
- Develop geographic questions about survival on the Petersons' journey.
- Calculate the distances traveled for each family member.
- Gather information about the cities through which the family traveled.
- Organize material on maps and charts.
- Analyze and explain the geographic information from the maps and charts.
- Develop and present a report comparing the cities in 1945 and today.

Perspectives

Recognize and appreciate the sacrifices and struggles the Petersons made in their journey to freedom. Understand that uncontrolled events may cause a separation of paths in one's life.

Activities

I = Individual   P = Pairs   G = Group

A. FREEDOM ROUTE (I)

Materials: globe, wall map of Europe, intermediate atlas, blank outline map of Europe, colored pencils, pencils, markers

Using the globe, locate Europe, noting the water and land forms in the areas through which the Petersons traveled. On the wall map, identify the countries through which the family passed. On the blank outline map of Europe, label the countries and the cities where they stayed. Include the country borders as they were in 1945. Plot the route in three different colors: red for when the family was together, violet for the family without Hugo, and orange for Hugo's route. Develop a legend showing the routes and colors. Label and color the water areas blue. Place a compass rose and scale of miles on the map.

Questions to Ask

1. Where did the Petersons begin their flight for freedom?
2. Through what countries and cities did the family members pass and live?
3. Following the different colored routes, using the scale of miles and the book as a guide, how many miles did the family members travel before they were reunited?
4. What land and water forms did they encounter on their journey?
5. Having read the book, and putting yourself in Hugo's and Astra's places, what views, images, and feelings would you have during the search for freedom?

B. Yesterday and Today (P)

Materials: atlas, encyclopedia, computer, Internet search, computerized database of magazines and journals

Pairs should choose a city on the Petersons' route to investigate. Gather information and pictures, where possible, concerning that city in 1945 and today. Organize the information according to demograph-ics, landmarks, and industries in bar graphs comparing present data to data from 1945. In a written report, draw conclusions regarding the destruction and reconstruction caused by political strife. Share reports with the class and discuss the impact of war on the selected cities in Europe.

C. Refugees' Routes (G)

Materials: atlas, encyclopedia, computer, Internet, *National Geographic* magazines, poster board, poster paints, marking pens, opaque projector or computer scanner

In groups, determine a region or state in the world that recently has been having political or other problems leading to refugee movement. Have each group choose one of these regions to research. Students should determine how the conditions of their choice are similar to or different from those of the Petersons' flight from Latvia. Using the atlas with the opaque projector or computer scanner, create a map of the area showing natural resources, physical features, political boundaries, and human-made structures. On the map, show the lines of refugee movement. Prepare an oral presentation based on inferences from the data that presents the impact of physical, political, and cultural geography as causes and effects of conflict leading to refugee movement.

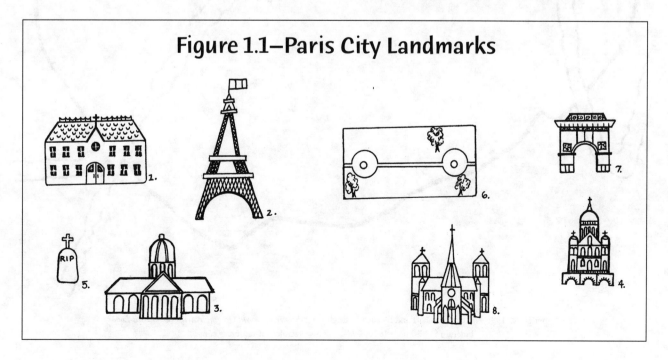

Figure 1.1—Paris City Landmarks

Figure 1.2–Paris City Map

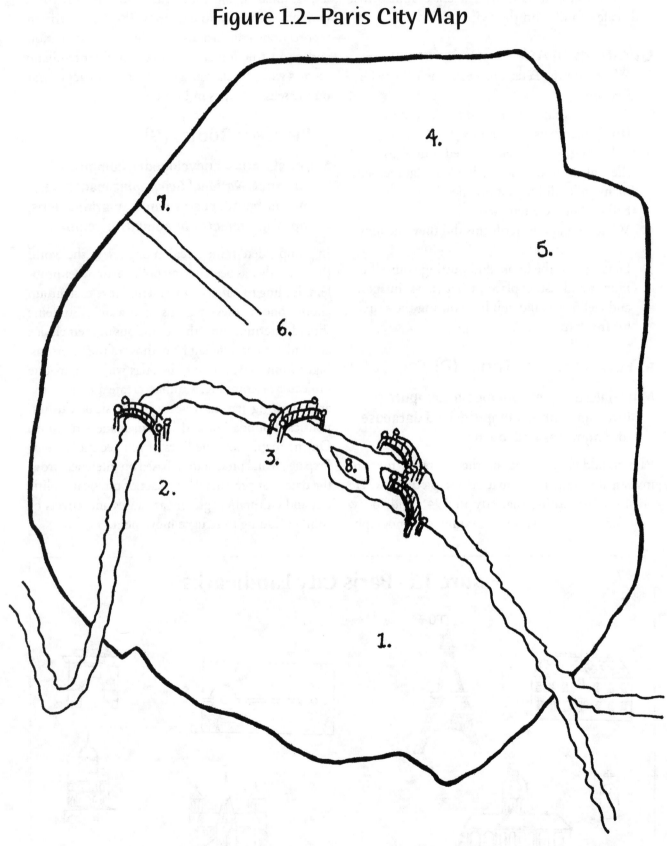

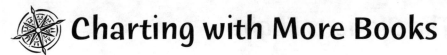

Charting with More Books

Golem

Projection: *Golem* by David Wisniewski, 1996
Genre: **Legend**
Level: **Intermediate (4–6)**
Elements: **II. Places and Regions; IV. Human Systems**
Themes: **Location; Place; Region; Human/Environment Interaction**

The Book

In sixteenth-century Prague, the Jews, victims of intolerance and slander, were kept in a walled ghetto. Fearing that violence was inevitable and praying for help, the chief rabbi dreamed of the word *golem*. Based on cabalistic teachings, a holy man could create and control a huge creature made of clay. The rabbi went to the riverbank at night and fashioned a giant clay figure. Through the rabbi's prayers, heavenly power changed the Golem into a man. The Golem was told that he was to stay human only until the Jews in Prague were safe.

When an angry mob attacked, the giant defeated it with a swipe of his huge hands. The emperor offered peace and protection to the Jews, provided that the rabbi destroyed the monster. Despite the pleas of the Golem to stay human, he was turned back to clay. He waits to fight for justice once again.

The Red Balloon

Projection: *The Red Balloon* by Albert Lamorisse, 1990
Genre: **Picture Storybook**
Level: **Bridge (2–4)**
Elements: **I. The World in Spatial Terms; II. Places and Regions**
Themes: **Location; Place**

The Book

Pascal was a lonely schoolboy living in Paris. One day he came upon a big red balloon tied to a street lamp. After he freed it, the magic balloon followed him wherever he went. Pascal and the balloon caused quite a stir in school, church, and on the street. Misadventure took place when a group of boys caught the balloon. Pascal rescued the balloon but was cornered by the boys, who began to throw stones at the two. He begged the balloon to fly away; it did not and was hit. All over Paris balloons began to fly, forming a long, colorful line. They all descended upon Pascal, who caught their strings and twisted them together. The balloons lifted Pascal high into the sky and took him on a trip around the globe.

The Glorious Flight

Projection:	*The Glorious Flight* by Alice and Martin Provensen, 1987
Genre:	Informational Picture Storybook
Level:	Primary (K–2)
Elements:	I. The World in Spatial Terms; II. Places and Regions
Themes:	Location; Place; Region

The Book

In 1901, in Cambrai, France, Louis Blériot saw his first airship and was determined not only to learn to fly but to build a plane as well. For five years he experimented with different Blériot airplane models with the same results: They all crashed. The Blériot XII was different, for it could fly. He decided to enter a competition for a prize of a thousand pounds offered for the first flight across the English Channel. On July 25, 1909, Blériot XII lifted off for England. With fog surrounding the plane, Blériot was unable to see and knew he was lost. Suddenly the fog lifted and the White Cliffs of Dover appeared. Louis Blériot had flown coast to coast in 37 minutes.

Strega Nona Meets Her Match

Projection:	*Strega Nona Meets Her Match* by Tomie dePaola, 1993
Genre:	Picture Storybook
Level:	Primary (K–2)
Elements:	I. The World in Spatial Terms; II. Places and Regions; IV. Human Systems
Themes:	Location; Place; Region

The Book

In Calabria, a small town in Italy, Strega Nona ("Grandma Witch") lived with Big Anthony and Bambolona. One day Strega Nona was visited by her friend Strega Amelia from the other side of the mountain. The visitor was impressed by the number of people who came to Strega Nona for advice and cures. Strega Amelia copied Strega Nona's methods and, in addition, used the latest scientific equipment and served sweets and cappuccino. As a result, most of the townspeople became Amelia's clients. Even Big Anthony accepted a job with Amelia and, as usual, proceeded to bungle the cures and equipment. The townspeople returned to Strega Nona. The mayor informed Amelia that the people preferred Strega Nona and the old ways. For once, Big Anthony was helpful to Strega Nona.

 Pepito's Story

Projection: *Pepito's Story* by Eugene Fern, 1991
Genre: **Picture Storybook**
Level: **Primary (K-2)**
Elements: **I. The World in Spatial Terms; II. Places and Regions; IV. Human Systems**
Themes: **Location; Place; Region**

The Book

A little Spanish boy, Pepito, lived in a small fishing village by the sea. He loved to dance, unlike the other children, who preferred to play by the sea. In this same town, high on the hill, lived a very rich but very sick young girl, Estrellita. To improve her spirits, she asked her father if she could see her friends who lived and played by the sea. The children all came to her bedside bearing gifts, but none were able to cheer up Estrellita. When Pepito entered the room, he carried no gift but rather delighted her with dance. She got out of bed and danced with Pepito. From that day on she enjoyed playing with her friends by the sea but maintained a special friendship with her dancing friend, Pepito.

Starry Messenger

Projection: *Starry Messenger* by Peter Sis, 1996
Genre: **Biography**
Level: **Bridge; Intermediate (2-6)**
Elements: **I. The World in Spatial Terms; II. Places and Regions; VI. The Uses of Geography**
Themes: **Location; Region; Human/Environment Interaction**

The Book

Disputing accepted religious beliefs and traditions through the use of observation and reason, Galileo Galilei proved that the earth was not the fixed center of the universe. This inquisitive stargazer, skilled in mathematics and physics, designed scientific instruments such as the thermometer, the compound microscope, and the telescope. With the latter instrument he was able to observe, in detail, the moon, galaxy, sun, and Jupiter with its revolving moons. His discoveries and mapping of the celestial bodies were published in his book, *Starry Messenger*. Immensely popular, read by kings and princesses and translated into many languages, the book brought great renown to the astronomer. The pope's court, however, found him guilty of heresy for the doctrine that the earth moved around the sun. Some 350 years later, the church pardoned Galileo, admitting that his courageous convictions had been correct.

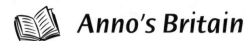 *Anno's Britain*

Projection:	*Anno's Britain* by Mitsumasa Anno, 1985
Genre:	Wordless Book
Level:	Primary; Bridge; Intermediate (K–6)
Elements:	I. The World in Spatial Terms; II. Places and Regions; IV. Human Systems
Themes:	Location; Place; Region

The Book

A sojourner travels to various locations throughout Britain in this uniquely illustrated book that blends time periods, famous characters, and events throughout. The author includes many of the important British landmarks (Windsor Castle, Saint Paul's Cathedral, London Bridge) and physical features (White Cliffs of Dover, canals, green pastures) along the way. Diverse occupations and pursuits are colorfully and creatively detailed. The reader will enjoy searching, from a bird's-eye view, for some of the more obscure cultural features of Britain. Each time this wordless book is viewed, new and different experiences may occur.

 *Persephone*

Projection:	*Persephone* by Warwick Hutton, 1994
Genre:	Picture Storybook, myth
Level:	Bridge (2–4)
Elements:	I. The World in Spatial Terms; III. Physical Systems
Themes:	Location; Place

The Book

According to Greek myth, the god Zeus ruled over the earth and heavens and Hades ruled the cold, dark underworld. Hades knew no nymph or goddess would willingly become queen of this barren place, so he decided to kidnap one. He chanced upon the beautiful nymph Persephone, the daughter of Demeter who was goddess of all growing things on Earth. He carried Persephone back to the underworld. Frightened and lonely without her mother and the warmth of the sun, Persephone wept continuously and ate nothing but six pomegranate seeds.

When Demeter discovered where her daughter was, she informed Zeus, who made Hades return the nymph, provided she had eaten nothing. Because Persephone had eaten the seeds, Zeus declared that she would spend half of the year with her mother, when the sun would shine and plants would grow, and the remaining six months in the dreary underworld, when nothing would grow while Demeter mourned her daughter's absence. Thus, the seasons came to be.

Kisses from Rosa

Projection: *Kisses from Rosa* by Petra Mathers, 1995
Genre: **Picture Storybook**
Level: **Primary (K–2)**
Elements: **I. The World in Spatial Terms; II. Places and Regions**
Themes: **Location; Place; Region**

The Book

Her mother was ill, so Rosa was sent to stay with her Aunt Mookie on a farm at the edge of the Black Forest in Germany. The homesick little girl was sad, for country life was very different from life in the city. At first only letters received from Mami, her mother, could make her happy. As time went by Rosa came to like helping her aunt with farm and house chores. She told about her activities in letters to her Mami in which she always sent special kisses. Just before Christmas a letter arrived with the news that Mami was well. Rosa was to come back home. Life on the farm had been good, but being with Mami was best.

Realm References

Anno, M. 1985. *Anno's Britain*. New York: Philomel Books.

Bemelmans, L. 1993. *Madeline's Rescue*. New York: Viking Penguin.

dePaola, T. 1993. *Strega Nona Meets Her Match*. New York: G. P. Putnam's Sons.

Farndon, J. 1994. *Dictionary of the Earth*. New York: DK Publishing.

Fern, E. 1991. *Pepito's Story*. New York: Bantam Books.

Hutton, W. 1994. *Persephone*. New York: Macmillan.

Kunhardt, E. 1987. *Pompeii … Buried Alive!* New York: Random House.

Lamorisse, A. 1990. *The Red Balloon*. New York: Delacorte Press.

Lingard, J. 1992. *Tug of War*. New York: Puffin Books.

Mathers, P. 1995. *Kisses from Rosa*. New York: Alfred A. Knopf.

Provensen, A., and M. Provensen. 1987. *The Glorious Flight*. New York: Puffin Books.

Sis, P. 1996. *Starry Messenger*. New York: Farrar, Straus and Giroux.

Wisniewski, D. 1996. *Golem*. New York: Clarion Books.

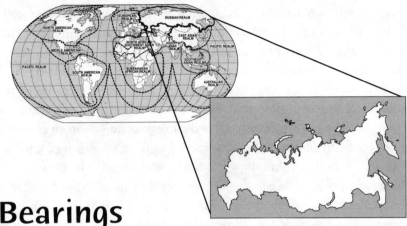

Chapter 2
Russian Realm

Getting Your Bearings

Location

Russia, the largest country in the world, makes up the Russian Realm, an area of 6,592,800 square miles. Spanning 6,000 miles east and west and 2,800 miles north and south, this massive realm contains four major regions: Russian Core, Siberia, Eastern Frontier, and Far East. Russia is located between 39°N and 82°N latitude and 28°E and 170°W longitude and is bordered by eastern Europe on the west, the Pacific Ocean on the east, the Arctic Ocean on the north, and the realms of North Africa/Southwest Asia and East Asia on the south. Moscow, the capital of Russia, is situated in the populous Russian Core. The population of 147,480,000 is mostly concentrated west of the Ural Mountains.

Topography

Several mountain ranges, including the Caucasus Mountains, the Ural Mountains, and the Eastern Highlands, which include the Sikhote-Alin' and the Verkhoyanski Mountains, are found in the Russian Realm. The Ural Mountains provide a natural boundary separating European Russia from Asian Russia. The highest peak in Russia (and in Europe) is Mount Elbrus, at 18,510 feet. The Russian Plain, which lies west of the Urals, is the heartland of this realm. East of the Urals lies the world's largest lowland, the West Siberian Plain. Bleak Siberia encompasses more than half of Russia. Lake Baykal, in the Eastern Frontier, is the deepest freshwater lake in the world. More than 395 miles in length and 37

miles across, it connects the republics of Irkutsk Oblast and Buryatia. The well-known Volga River, which is in the Russian Core, travels 2,193 miles from northwest of Moscow to the Caspian Sea.

Climate

With a very cold, dry climate, Russia may be viewed as having only two seasons, winter and summer. Snow is a prominent feature of the Russian climate, and latitude and altitude influence the duration of snow cover, which ranges from 40 to 250 days, based on location. Spring and fall are only brief transitions to the other seasons. Russia's large land mass, located away from the moderating influence of large bodies of water, contributes to the harsh climate, with extreme temperatures in winter and summer. The temperatures vary greatly within the regions. In winter, for example, Saint Petersburg averages -17°F and Verkhoyansk averages -58°F, with a record low of -94°F. In the summer temperatures can rise to an average of 39°F in the Arctic regions and 68°F in the south.

Flora and Fauna

Four main zones across Russia, from north to south, are influenced by climatic and soil conditions: (1) the tundra, (2) the forest (taiga), (3) the steppes, and (4) the semidesert and mountainous zone. On the tundra, an area largely influenced by permafrost, plant life is sparse, including mosses and lichens and low shrubs. Among the animals found here are reindeer,

Arctic fox, beaver, lemming, and ptarmigan. The taiga is located south of the tundra and encompasses the world's largest reserve of coniferous and mixed forests. The taiga is the habitat for sable, ermine, elk and deer, wolf, brown bear, and the fast-disappearing lynx. The steppes are primarily grassy plains bordered on the north by wooded plains, whose rich soil and climatic conditions have contributed to the conversion of grassy areas to agriculture. Antelope, rodents, and small burrowing animals live in the steppes; birds include bustards, eagles, and kestrels. The semidesert and mountainous zone is home to desertlike vegetation near the Caspian Sea and lush vegetation in the mild climate of the Caucasus Mountains.

Unique Features

Because of the vast expanse of land in the Russian Federation, eleven time zones can be passed through on an east-west journey. The Trans-Siberian Railroad is well known for its long, tedious trek across Russia from west to east. The realm's eighty-nine political divisions are inhabited by diverse racial, ethnic, religious, and cultural groups, including Asians, Caucasians, Ukrainians, Tartars, Turks, and Muslims.

 # Mapping

 ## *Anastasia's Album*

Projection:	*Anastasia's Album* by Hugh Brewster, 1996
Genre:	Information Book; Photographic Biography
Level:	Intermediate (4–6)
Elements:	I. The World in Spatial Terms; II. Places and Regions; IV. Human Systems
Themes:	Location; Region; Human/Environment Interaction

The Book

The youngest daughter of Tsar Nicholas II of Russia, Anastasia, in photographs and letters, tells the story of her life and that of her family, the Romanovs. In chapters designated by time periods in her short life, the reader is introduced to Anastasia, born in 1901, and follows her life through her execution in 1918. The wealth of the Romanovs provided a privileged existence for Anastasia, her three sisters, and her younger brother. The family shuttled among five magnificent palaces and cruised the Baltic Sea on a floating palace, the *Standart*.

Throughout her life the beautiful Grand Duchess Anastasia showed evidence of artistic talent and humor. Her creativity is shown in the way she added color to the family photographs and in the artistic backgrounds she designed for the photo album. She also played jokes on family members and did witty imitations of palace visitors.

After the Russian Revolution the Romanovs were taken by Red Army officials and hidden in a variety of locations in Russia. Life as a prisoner made Anastasia's remaining days humiliating and difficult. Eleven days before a planned rescue by the White Army, Anastasia and her family were shot and their bodies burned and buried.

Key Understandings

The constant struggle for control of the earth's surface results in changing power, boundaries, and lifestyles. The Russian Revolution brought about the brutal end of the royal rule of the Romanovs.

Knowledge

- Locate Russia and the habitats of the Romanov family.
- Describe the life of the Romanov family.

- Detail the activities of Grand Duchess Anastasia.
- Compare the lifestyle of Tsar Nicholas and his family to that of the general Russian population.
- Explain the consequences of the dichotomy of the two lifestyles.

Skills

- Ask questions about the location of Russia and that of the tsar's family.
- Ask questions about the Romanovs and the Russian people during this time period.
- Gather information about the Russian Revolution, Russian rulers and leaders, and the Russian people.
- Organize information into maps and a personal photo album.
- Analyze the data according to the location and sequence of events and activities of Romanov family life.
- Formulate conclusions about the causes of the Russian Revolution and the demise of the Romanov family.

Perspectives

Value the idea that power must be used to enrich the lives of everyone, especially when ruling vast areas. Recognize that the location and size of Russia and the lifestyle of the Romanovs contributed to the rise of Communism.

Activities

I = Individual   P = Pairs   G = Group

A. Arriving at Anastasia's World (I)

Materials: wall map of Eurasia, map from p. 63 of *Anastasia's Album*, atlas, tracing paper, drawing paper, pencils, colored pencils, marking pens

On the wall map, locate today's Russia and note the political boundaries. Look at the map on p. 63 of *Anastasia's Album* and compare the political boundaries during the reign of Tsar Nicholas II, describing

variations. Using tracing paper, trace the outline of modern Russia. Transfer the outline to white drawing paper. Add the boundary from Tsar Nicholas II's time, which included present-day Ukraine, Belarus, Lithuania, Latvia, Estonia, and Finland in eastern Europe and some countries in southwest Asia. Mark the Caspian, Black, and Baltic Seas and the Ural Mountains. Students should identify and locate on their maps the old capital, Saint Petersburg, and other cities where Anastasia and her family resided. Add the Trans-Siberian Railroad and appropriate colors for land and water. Include a map title, scale of miles, and compass rose.

Questions to Ask

1. What countries border Russia today?
2. What countries bordered Russia before the revolution?
3. In terms of location and size, how is prerevolutionary Russia different from Russia today?
4. Where did the Romanovs live?
5. What are the distances between the palace at Saint Petersburg and the other palaces?
6. How far on the Trans-Siberian Railroad did Anastasia travel to reach the end of the Romanov line in Ekaterinburg?
7. What can you conclude about the isolation of the royal family in relation to the population of this vast area?

B. In Anastasia's Shoes: A Readers' Theatre (G)

Materials: computer/word processor, chairs/stools, paper, music stands (optional), color highlighters, Reader's Theatre reproducible

Each group of four to five students must choose a segment of the book to dramatize a time period or a special event. Each group then creates a script that includes a dialogue and an epilogue. On the Reader's Theatre reproducible (Figure 2.1 on page 22), create an introduction and a diagram of placement of actors. The introduction, consisting of the setting, character description, and players; the epilogue; and

Colorizing the photos.

c. AN ALBUM FOR ANASTASIA AND ME (I)

d. **Materials:** 8.5 x 11-inch piece of white construction paper, oil pastels, one-hole punch, glue stick, photocopy paper, copier, copy of the book, personal photos, pen, computer/word processor, ribbon or metal rings

Students gather personal photographs that relate to various time periods in their lives. Choose pictures to be photocopied from *Anastasia's Album* and personal collections that are comparable. On construction paper, arrange and glue pictures side by side so that Anastasia's life can be compared to the student's life. Students should add designs to each page and, using the oil pastels, add color to the photographs. Script and personal letters may be added. Create a cover that includes a title and appropriate design. The cover should be laminated before the book is bound. Students punch holes and bind their books with ribbon or a metal ring. Students share their albums with others, describing how their lives are alike or different from Anastasia's. Display the albums.

a concluding statement must be read by the narrator. Once written, the play should be word processed in a large font, at least double-spaced. Cast members should each receive a final copy of the script to highlight their roles. Each group should practice reading the script to ensure dramatic emphasis. Set up chairs and stools according to placement diagram. Use the music stands to hold the scripts. Students present the readers' theatre production.

The Fool of the World and the Flying Ship

Projection:	*The Fool of the World and the Flying Ship* retold by Arthur Ransome, 1991
Genre:	Folktale
Level:	Bridge (2–4)
Elements:	I. The World in Spatial Terms; II. Places and Regions
Themes:	Location; Place

The Book

The czar of Russia announced that he would give his daughter in marriage to anyone who could bring him a flying ship. Although he did not know how to make one, a young, simple peasant man called the "Fool of the World" set out to wed the princess. He met an old man and, because he was kind to everyone, he shared his meager food with him. The old man rewarded the fool with a flying ship, which the fool sailed high above the trees. On his way to the palace, he picked up several amiable shipmates, each with a special talent or magic object. Angry that a peasant should wish to wed his daughter, the czar set up tasks that were all but impossible to perform. However, the fool's mates helped him complete each task so he could wed the princess.

Key Understandings

Russia is so vast a realm that it includes eleven time zones. This huge area encompasses a variety of climates and topography.

One's kind deeds are often repaid in strange and wonderful ways.

Knowledge

- Describe the characteristics of time zones.
- Identify the locations of the eleven time zones in Russia.
- Identify the topography and climate from a flying-ship view.
- Compare the time zones in the United States to those in Russia.

Skills

- Ask questions about the topography and climate of Russia.
- Ask questions about the configuration of the time zones throughout Russia.
- Gather information about a hypothetical east-west trip across Russia that includes topography, climate, and time zones.
- Organize information about topography and climate for each of the time zones.
- Formulate conclusions concerning the impact the size of Russia has on the lives of the people.

Perspectives

Appreciate the vastness of Russia and the patterns of habitation that result.

Activities

I = Individual   P = Pairs   G = Group

A. FOOL'S TRAVEL THROUGH TIME (P)

Materials: atlas, globe, wall map, time zones of the world, outline map of Russia, pencils, markers, *Somewhere in the World Right Now* by Stacey Schuett

Using the atlas, globe, and wall map, locate Russia, noting its extent. Look for the variety of land and water features shown on a topographical map. On the world map, locate the eleven time zones. Find Saint Petersburg and Petropavlovsk-Kamchatskiy for use on the outline map. Draw in the time zones, taking care to follow the lines around topographical features. Place the two cities on the time-zone map.

Questions to Ask

1. When it is noon in Petropavlovsk-Kamchatskiy, what time is it in Saint Petersburg? Is Saint Petersburg to the west or east of Petropavlovsk-Kamchatskiy? So will it be earlier or later in Saint Petersburg?
2. How many time zones are there between these two cities? Traveling west, how many time zones are there between Moscow and Washington, DC?
3. What mountain ranges can you find in the time zones?
4. What bodies of water do you find?
5. Considering the number of time zones and the varied topography, what would a trip across Russia be like?

B. THE FOOL'S MAP (G)

Materials: plain white window shade, pencils, markers (all colors), opaque projector, time-zone map, tape

The teacher should provide an opaque projector and a time-zone map of Russia. The window shade should be opened to its fullest extent and taped horizontally to a wall or chalkboard. Project the map onto the shade and trace the outline of Russia and its eleven time zones. Once this is completed, assign approximately two time zones per group. Have each group fill in the topographical features for the assigned time zones. Once completed, add a compass rose and title to the map. Display the map for all groups to view.

C. THE FOOL'S TALE (G)

Materials: pencils, paper, a flying ship

Using the time zones assigned by the teacher in the previous activity, have students plot a journey. Beginning with the first group at Petropavlovsk-Kamchatskiy, plot the route of the flying ship. Have the second and subsequent groups pick up their routes from the point where the previous group ended. Continue this format for all groups until the czar's palace at Saint Petersburg is reached. Each group is responsible for creating a tale that focuses on a particular topographical feature (e.g., Lake Baykal, Ural Mountains) in its respective time zone. During a class presentation, have each group present its tale as the flying ship crosses time zones. Have students place replicas of the flying ship within the time zones to correspond with the content of their tales. Once the czar's palace is reached, the flying ships will reveal the fool's route across Russia. Now that the goal has been reached, have students agree upon a most fanciful imaginary reward.

 # Russian Girl: Life in an Old Russian Town

Projection:	*Russian Girl: Life in an Old Russian Town* by Russ Kendall, 1994
Genre:	Information Book
Level:	Bridge; Intermediate (2–6)
Elements:	I. The World in Spatial Terms; II. Places and Regions; IV. Human Systems
Themes:	Location; Place; Region

The Book

The reader is provided with a photographic view of Olga Surikova, who lives with her family in the thousand-year-old town of Suzdal in western Russia near Moscow. The pictures and text show nine-year-old Olga at work and play against a background of medieval traditions.

Olga is depicted in her third-grade class. She is excited about learning English, for she hopes to visit America someday. Her school tasks also include taking part in serving students their lunch. After school she helps her babushka (grandmother) with farm chores such as milking cows and collecting eggs. During her winter school holiday in November, Olga and her family build snow figures and prepare a special dinner celebration for her father's namesake saint's day.

The book includes an informational section on recipes, alphabet, vocabulary, and the history of Suzdal and Russia.

Key Understandings

The daily lives of people in Russia are influenced by location, climate, and tradition. Children in this huge nation adapt to their environment in ways that reflect hardship, joy, and pleasure, as do children of all nations.

Knowledge

- Identify the absolute and relative locations of Olga's medieval town.
- Describe the typical events in the daily life of Olga and her family.
- Depict the occupations of Olga's family.
- Compare and contrast Olga's daily life to your own.

Skills

- Ask questions about the location and climate of Suzdal in Russia.
- Ask questions about the events and traditions in the life of Olga and her family.

- Find information and pictures in the atlases and encyclopedias about villages and towns in western Russia.
- Organize the information into a chronological timeline.
- Interpret how location and climate affect a day in the life of a Russian child.
- Formulate conclusions about similarities and differences in the lives of a Russian child and an American child.

Perspectives

Appreciate how lives are shaped by the spatial and cultural patterns of the locale.

Activities

I = Individual   P = Pairs   G = Group

A. OLGA'S OLD RUSSIAN TOWN (I)

Materials: atlas, globe, wall maps

Have students find the absolute location of Suzdal, noting longitude and latitude. Next, discover and report the relative location of Suzdal, including points within and outside Russia. Find communities in North America that are at the same latitude. Compare climatic conditions.

Questions to Ask
1. What is the absolute location of Suzdal?
2. What is its relative location?
3. What countries and/or communities in North America share the same latitude as Suzdal?
4. What is the climate like in Suzdal and in another community in North America at the same latitude?
5. How would this climate affect your life? How does the climate affect Olga?

B. OVERVIEW OF OLGA'S DAY TIMELINE (I)

Materials: poster board, markers, yardstick/ruler, white glue, pictures, scissors, travel and geographic magazines

Collect pictures of western Russia that are typical of small-town life. Organize the pictures according to activities that a Russian child would be engaged in at different times of the day. Create a vertical timeline from wake-up to bedtime. Label the activities in the appropriate time slots. Glue in pictures that graphically depict the activities. For some activities, students may have to draw and color, since pictures may be unavailable. Title the timeline and present it to the class, comparing activities in which they would be engaged at the same time as Olga.

C. MEDIEVAL TASTE TREAT (G)

Materials: recipe for pirog on page 35 of *Russian Girl*, cooking utensils, oven, oven mitts, cutting board, paper plates, forks, cups, cold milk, 3 x 5-inch cards, markers

Make a copy of the pirog recipe for each group of students. Distribute the recipe, ingredients, and utensils to each group of four to five students. Students should divide tasks equally and complete the recipe. Each group can then share the pirog with friends from another class. Fold the 3 x 5-inch cards in half and use them as name cards. Have each student reformulate his or her own name according to the directions on page 37 of *Russian Girl* and write the patronymic on the card. When the friends from the other class arrive for the pirog and milk, their partners in the group will help to create a patronymic name card for them. During the "Medieval Taste Treat," only patronymic names should be used.

Figure 2.1—In Anastasia's Shoes: A Readers' Theatre

Introduction:

Diagram of Actors:

Charting with More Books

 ## *Babushka Baba Yaga*

Projection:	*Babushka Baba Yaga* retold by Patricia Polacco, 1993
Genre:	Folktale
Level:	Primary (K–2)
Elements:	I. The World in Spatial Terms; II. Places and Regions
Themes:	Location; Place

The Book

The horrible forest creature Baba Yaga, feared by children and adults, was, in reality, a lonely woman longing to be a *babushka* with a grandchild. Disguising her pointed ears with a traditional scarf, Baba Yaga got to take care of a little boy, Victor. As his *babushka*, she taught the boy about the forest and its creatures. Overhearing stories of the bad Baba Yaga, Victor was frightened. Baba Yaga knew it was time to leave. Later Baba Yaga emerged from the forest to save Victor from wolves, and because of this she was finally referred to in a loving way as Babushka Baba Yaga.

 ## *The Little Humpbacked Horse*

Projection:	*The Little Humpbacked Horse* adapted by Elizabeth Winthrop, 1997
Genre:	Folktale
Level:	Bridge (2–4)
Elements:	I. The World in Spatial Terms; II. Places and Regions
Themes:	Location; Place

The Book

Ivan, a peasant, captured a white mare with a long, curly golden mane. To gain her freedom, the mare gave Ivan three colts. Two were brown and gray with golden manes and fit for the tsar, while the other was a short, two-humped pony with long ears. Although strange looking, this small colt was very wise. The two handsome colts so pleased the tsar that Ivan was made master of the stables. Jealous of the new royal favorite, the courtiers plotted against him, and the tsar forced Ivan to undertake impossible tasks that only the little horse could help him complete. Because of his success, Ivan became the tsar, married the beautiful tsarevna, and ruled the country for a long time.

 *Rechenka's Eggs*

Projection:	*Rechenka's Eggs* by Patricia Polacco, 1988
Genre:	Picture Storybook
Level:	Primary (K–2)
Elements:	I. The World in Spatial Terms; II. Places and Regions
Themes:	Location; Place

The Book

Babushka worked during the cold Russian winter painting eggs for the *Moskva* festival. She found a wounded goose that she named Rechenka and took care of it. In gratitude, Rechenka laid an egg in her basket every morning for Babushka's breakfast. One day the goose accidentally broke the painted eggs, which made Babushka very sad. For the next twelve mornings, she found beautifully painted eggs in the basket, which were judged the most beautiful in the festival. Before she flew away, Rechenka left another egg from which came a little goose, her parting gift to Babushka.

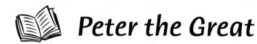 *Peter the Great*

Projection:	*Peter the Great* by Diane Stanley, 1986
Genre:	Biography
Level:	Bridge; Intermediate (2–6)
Elements:	I. The World in Spatial Terms; II. Places and Regions; V. Environment and Society
Themes:	Location; Place; Region; Human/Environment Interaction

The Book

Tsar Peter spent his growing years pampered, isolated, and curious about the world outside Russia. He was fascinated by European modern dress, customs, advancements in science, and, his favorite, ship building. As no other tsar had ever done, Peter not only visited European countries but also went as a common pupil, observing, learning, and even working as a ship builder. He returned with skilled people, technical objects, and plans to build a modern country with its own navy and a seaport. The latter was achieved when he built the seaport city of beautiful buildings and bridges named Saint Petersburg. Peter started Russia on its first steps toward becoming a powerful nation.

The Little Snowgirl

Projection:	*The Little Snowgirl* retold by Carolyn Croll, 1996
Genre:	Folktale
Level:	Primary (K–2)
Elements:	II. Places and Regions; IV. Human Systems
Themes:	Place; Region

The Book

Caterina and Pavel longed for a child. Christmas was a particularly sad time for them. Pavel built a snowgirl as a surprise gift for his wife. When the little girl magically came to life, Caterina had her Dochinka, "Little Daughter," at last. Unlike real girls, the snowgirl could never be near or eat anything hot, for she would melt. On Christmas Eve the couple carried the sleeping snowgirl indoors, and to their sorrow nothing was left in the morning but a puddle. To their joy, Babushka, who gave good children their Christmas wishes, had turned the child of snow into a real girl.

Realm References

Brewster, H. 1996. *Anastasia's Album*. New York: Hyperion Books for Children.

Croll, C. 1996. *The Little Snowgirl*. New York: The Putnam and Grosset Group.

Kendall, R. 1994. *Russian Girl: Life in an Old Russian Town*. New York: Scholastic.

Polacco, P. 1988. *Rechenka's Eggs*. New York: Philomel Books.

——. 1993. *Babushka Baba Yaga*. New York: Philomel Books.

Ransome, A. 1991. *The Fool of the World and the Flying Ship*. New York: Farrar, Straus and Giroux.

Schuett, S. 1995. *Somewhere in the World Right Now*. New York: Alfred A. Knopf.

Stanley, D. 1986. *Peter the Great*. New York: Four Winds Press.

Winthrop, E. 1997. *The Little Humpbacked Horse*. New York: Clarion Press.

Chapter 3
North American Realm

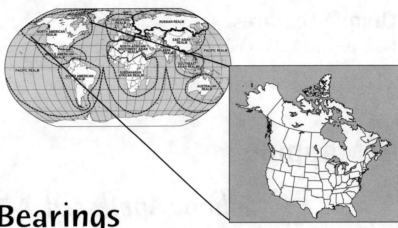

 Getting Your Bearings

Location

The North American Realm, located in the Western Hemisphere, is bounded by three oceans: the Arctic on the north, the Pacific on the west, and the Atlantic on the east. In the north, Canada, the second largest of all the North American nations, has the world's longest coastline and spans 3,849,670 square miles. Divided politically into ten provinces and two territories, its capital is Ottawa. To the south lie the forty-eight contiguous states of the United States. Alaska, the forty-ninth U.S. state, is situated to the northwest of Canada. With Washington, DC, as its capital, the United States encompasses 3,618,770 square miles. North America is situated between 83°N and 25°N latitude and 170°W to 50°W longitude.

Topography

The tundra proceeds across Canada and Alaska and around the Arctic Circle. There are two major mountain ranges: the Appalachian Mountains, which extend from Newfoundland in the north to Georgia in the south, and the Rocky Mountains, which extend north to south from Alaska to the Mexican border. Scoured out by glaciers, the Great Lakes are shared by both countries. Among the numerous rivers, two are outstanding: the Saint Lawrence, a major shipping lane that flows through the Canadian provinces of Ontario and Quebec and borders the United States in New York state, and the Mississippi, the lifeline of the central United States. The Canadian Shield, composed of heavily glaciated, barren land, stretches from the Atlantic Ocean to the Yukon. On the southwestern side of the shield begin the Great Plains, which extend southward into the United States.

Climate

Although a generally temperate climate predominates, temperatures range in January from an average low of around -12°F on the Arctic Circle to average highs of 50°F in the southwestern United States. Summer temperatures range from 68°F in the north to 123°F in the desert Southwest. A desert climate is found between the Rocky Mountains and the Sierra Nevadas from Idaho to Arizona. A warm, humid, subtropical climate can be found in Florida.

Flora and Fauna

Animals found in the Arctic area include polar bears, walruses, caribou, and puffins. In the desert Southwest, armadillos, gila monsters, and a variety of rattlesnakes are found. Alligators are found in the southeast United States. Mountain lions, lynx, and bobcats are the most notable members of the cat family. The buffalo that once roamed the Great Plains in millions have been reduced to protected herds on a few reserves and ranches. The vegetation varies across this extensive region as well. There are vast regions of tundra in northern Canada and Alaska, great redwoods and giant firs in the Pacific Northwest, cacti and sagebrush in the western desert regions, and mangrove swamps in the Florida Everglades. In addition there are huge resident and migratory bird populations.

Unique Features

North America includes two of the world's most powerful industrialized nations and a wide variety of ethnic groups. Both Canada and the United States have allowed immigration from all nations, resulting in a conglomeration of European, African, Asian, and Hispanic peoples integrating with the indigenous population of native North Americans.

 # Mapping

 ## *Johnny Appleseed*: A Tall Tale

Projection:	*Johnny Appleseed: A Tall Tale* retold and illustrated by Steven Kellogg, 1996
Genre:	Folktale
Level:	Bridge; Intermediate (2–6)
Elements:	I. The World in Spatial Terms; II. Places and Regions; III. Physical Systems; V. Environment and Society
Theme:	Location; Movement

The Book

The retelling of the Johnny Appleseed tale begins with his birth in Vermont and relates his adventures until his death in Indiana seventy-four years later. John Chapman (his birth name) grew up on a farm in Massachusetts, where he came to appreciate not only the beauty of the blossoming apple orchard but also the ways that apples could be used to feed his family.

When he was older he left home to explore the wilderness of the West, taking along a bag of apple seeds. In his travels, he cleared the land and planted orchards. The resulting apples and apple saplings were used by the pioneers in their new settlements. The settlers passed on stories of Appleseed's work and adventures. So vivid and exaggerated were these tales that Johnny Appleseed remains a legend to this day.

Key Understandings

Personal perceptions of a region are based on one's culture and experience. The legacy of Johnny Appleseed, based on his perceptions of beauty and practicality, can be viewed and valued today in the multitude of apple orchards throughout the Northeast and Midwest.

Knowledge

- Identify regions east of the Mississippi, noting soil and climatic conditions beneficial for growing apples.
- Compare and contrast the economics of apple growing of the early nineteenth century with the economics of the present day.
- Describe how the apple has become an integral part of our modern culture.

Skills

- Create a list of questions concerning the following: location, soil conditions, and climate necessary for planting and maintaining apple orchards; the economics of apple growing; and the significance of the apple in U.S. culture.
- Collect data on the variety of apples available to the consumer. Gather information about the conditions for growing, buying, and selling apples.
- Make a graph representing the data collected. Trace or draw a regional map of Johnny Appleseed's journey west.
- Use a graph to explain apple production. Use the map to draw inferences concerning the legacy of Johnny Appleseed.

• Generalize the importance of apples in our culture.

Perspectives

Appreciate and nurture the resources in nature. Recognize the importance of personal contributions to the good of society. Acknowledge the economic impact of producing and exchanging goods.

Activities

I= Individual   P= Pairs   G= Group

A. JOHNNY'S JOURNEY (I, P, G)

Materials: map showing New England, the Mid-Atlantic states, and Indiana; newsprint or tagboard; poster paints and water-soluble marking pens

Trace Johnny's journey from his home in New England to the Midwest, noting direction, distance, and boundaries on the map provided, or hand draw a map with symbols and colors for natural geography features such as lakes (blue) or trees (green). Make the maps accurate and complete, including such items as title, compass rose, and key.

Questions to Ask

1. What direction did Johnny travel?
2. Through what states did he travel?
3. What were some of the water and land forms that he traversed on his journey?
4. What climatic conditions in this region were appropriate to apple growing?

B. JOHNNY'S JOURNAL (I)

Materials: notebook, pencil

Following the trail blazed by Johnny on the map in the previous activity, create a daily journal that might have been written by him about his observations of the natural environment and descriptions of situations in which he found himself. Include Johnny's feelings about what he saw and what he did.

C. APPLENOMICS (G)

Materials: clipboard, paper, pens and marking pens, graph paper, crayons, tape recorder

Determine what varieties of apples are sold at a large local supermarket, with each observing and recording the number of consumers buying one or more varieties of apples during a specific time period (minimum 30 minutes). A member of each group must ask about and record consumers' reasons for buying a particular variety.

Using data collected, collaborate to create a graph showing each variety of apple with the number of consumers buying a particular type. Contact the same supermarket to compare data collected to the market's data about consumer preferences. Determine the accuracy of your data-gathering survey.

 # Sweet Clara and the Freedom Quilt

Projection:	*Sweet Clara and the Freedom Quilt* by Deborah Hopkins, 1995
Genre:	**Historical Fiction**
Level:	**Intermediate (4–6)**
Elements:	**I. The World in Spatial Terms; II. Places and Regions; IV. Human Systems**
Themes:	**Location; Place; Movement**

The Book

Clara, a young slave girl and seamstress, heard about an underground railroad that would get slaves to freedom in a place called Canada. What was needed was a map to guide them.

She decided to sew a permanent map into the patterns of a quilt with leftover scraps of colored materials to serve as map symbols. Other slaves, whenever they were taken by their masters to places beyond the plantation, reported to Clara the land forms and objects they had observed. Clara cut and sewed their discoveries into her quilt map.

When it was completed, Clara committed her work to memory, leaving the quilt map behind to guide others to freedom in the North.

Key Understandings

Maps are guides to find specific locations. Freedom is a value desired by all people who are enslaved; those who have been enslaved will persevere in their attempts to gain freedom.

Knowledge

- Identify terms related to location and direction.
- Recognize symbols that represent features on a map.
- Compare and contrast the environment of a slave girl in the American South with a modern girl's environment.

Skills

- Develop a list of questions concerning the probable physical geography of the route mapped on Clara's quilt.
- Gather and organize data concerning the physical geography of Clara's route to Canada.
- Analyze the data to determine the easiest route for the underground railroad.
- Create a map of the route that best answers the questions posed.

Perspectives

Value the importance of maps to facilitate the movement of people and objects. Appreciate and care about freedom for all people.

Activities

I = Individual   P = Pairs   G = Group

A. Quilt Mapping (G)

Materials: projections of Canada and the United States as of the 1850s, 5 x 8-inch cards, marking pens, one-hole punch, masking tape, graph paper with outline map, various colors of knitting wool

Carefully observe Clara's quilt, noting different colored symbols and the route sewn by her. Using Clara's quilt with symbols as an example, create a map of your own route to freedom. Each group should select a southern state as a possible starting point for the freedom journey. Using old maps of the United States and Canada, determine the safest route to freedom based upon physical and human geography.

To make the quilt, cut twenty 5 x 8-inch cards into 5-inch squares for each group. Punch holes in each card, one at each corner and two others on each side equidistant from the corners. Place a small piece of rolled tape in the center of each card. On a large, flat surface align the cards four across and five down so that the sides are touching, forming a grid. In the top right corner create a compass rose. Using your freedom-map grid, transfer all features to the quilt grid, identifying political features (countries, states, capitals) and physical features. Color all features, following Clara's pattern. Working from top to bottom, beginning at the left edge, loop the yarn over and under through each hole, leaving about 3 inches extra at either end. Tie knots at both ends. Remove tape from the first column of sewn cards. Loop the yarn between the holes of the first column and the holes of the second column again, knotting the ends. Repeat this process for columns 3 and 4. Sew the right edge of column 5 to the left edge of column 1. Follow the same process for sewing and knotting the five rows. Title and hang the quilts for display. After reviewing both Clara's quilt and the freedom map, answer the following questions.

Questions to Ask

1. What was Clara's guiding point for direction? How would this help the slaves find their way north?
2. How does your route compare to Clara's route (e.g., symbols, features, colors)?

3. Could Clara have followed the quilt of your route? Explain.

B. MY FAMILY MAP (I)

Materials: Mercator projection of the globe, water-soluble marking pens, two colors of yarn, and pushpins

With colored yarns, trace on a Mercator projection a personal history path from one family's origins to its present U.S. location, including time frames, name notations, and pictures, if available, along the path. Make a list of questions for an interview with any living family members or review any written records to gather and verify information for the map.

C. FLIGHT FOR FREEDOM (P)

Materials: poster board, water-soluble marking pens, spinner or die, 3 x 5-inch cards, cardboard for cutout game pieces

On a poster board, design a decision-making board game titled "Flight for Freedom" based on the events

Plotting our family "routes."

told within the story. Include game pieces that relate to the characters, a spinner or a die, and obstacles that include open-ended decision-making vignettes (two- to three-sentence stories) that determine whether the character will be captured or waylaid or will continue on to victory—freedom.

 # The Backyard Birds of Summer

Projection:	*The Backyard Birds of Summer* by Carol Lerner, 1996
Genre:	**Information Book**
Level:	**Bridge; Intermediate (2–6; activities adaptable for K–1)**
Elements:	**I. The World in Spatial Terms; II. Places and Regions; III. Physical Systems; VI. The Uses of Geography**
Themes:	**Location; Place; Region; Human/Environment Interaction**

The Book

The variety of birds that migrate in the summer to North America from Middle or South America or from warmer locales in the United States are the focus of this book. They make this journey to mate, nest, and raise their young. The colorfully illustrated visitors are classified into feeder birds or those using houses. The male and female birds in each group are presented with their identifying characteristics, region of origin and residence, physical features, and feeding behavior.

Suggestions are provided on attracting birds into the backyard, building birdhouses, maintaining clean habitats, and feeding different species. The possible future loss of species' habitats due to the destruction of forests, agricultural use of the land, and an increase in human population is noted.

For summer birdwatchers, the book offers map inserts of the locations of migrating birds, making it easier for adults and children to identify and care for their feathered friends.

Key Understandings

Certain species of birds migrate with seasonal changes to warmer climates for survival. The environment must be preserved to support healthy bird populations. Humans can play an important role in maintaining migrant bird populations.

Knowledge

- Identify the regions in North America where feeder birds and birds that use houses are located.
- Describe the physical features, migration patterns, and eating habits of the migrant birds.
- Demonstrate how to support the local migrant bird populations.
- Compare and contrast various environments and their impact on the migrant birds.

Skills

- Pose questions about place of origin, habitat, behavior, identifying characteristics, and migration patterns.
- Locate and gather information from a variety of sources, including the Internet, the library, the Audubon Society, and local birdwatchers' groups.
- Categorize information for feeder birds and for birds that use houses.
- Using maps and charts, analyze the role of the environment and its impact upon bird behavior and migration patterns.
- Based on the information gathered, draw conclusions about migration patterns, habitat, and behavior of birds.

Perspectives

Value the delicate environmental relationships that support bird habitats. Believe that humans share a responsibility for protecting and fostering migrant bird populations.

Activities

I = Individual   P = Pairs   G = Group

A. Flying to the Summer Places (I)

Materials: student atlas, the book map for the bird selected, blank outline map of North America, white construction paper, scissors, white glue, colored marking pens, crayons

Adopt your favorite bird from the book. On the construction paper, draw and color two small pictures of your bird and cut them out. Using the outline map, trace the migratory route of your bird from its winter home to its summer place. Color in the region of this summer home. Glue the two pictures of the bird on its winter and summer homes. Include both a title (with your bird's name) and a compass rose on your map.

Questions to Ask

1. Where is your bird's winter place? Where is its summer place?
2. What countries/regions does your bird fly over to get to its summer place? What kinds of land forms does it fly over to reach its destination? What land forms are at its destination?
3. What is the climate like in its summer place?
4. What plant life is found there?
5. What other summer birds may be found there?
6. In what ways (habitat, behavior, etc.) do these birds differ from your adopted bird?

B. Feathered Friends Fete (I)

Materials: shallow pan, water, plastic milk or water container, scissors, twine, small pointed screw, birdseed

Place the shallow pan with water on the ground or on top of an inverted pail so birds can drink from and bathe in it. Make the feeder. (See Figure 3.1 on page 33.) Fill the feeder with the type of seeds that are preferred by the types of birds found in the area. Hang the feeder in an appropriate, observable area.

C. Birdwatchers' Journal (I)

Materials: notebook, pen or pencil, binoculars (if available)

In the journal, keep a record of the birds that choose to eat, drink, and bathe at the "Feathered Friends Fete." Record the identifying features (written descriptions and drawings) of the visiting birds, including coloring, size, and shape. Using a bird guide as a reference, name as many visiting birds as possible. Write your observations of their behaviors at the feeding and watering places. Describe the environmental factors that are attractive to the birds. Describe the environmental factors that are harmful to bird life. Upon returning to school, share the results of the birdwatching experience.

FEATHERED FRIENDS FEEDER

Directions: Gather the necessary materials. (For directions 2, 3, and 5, adult supervision is needed.)

1. Wash and dry the container. Replace the cap securely.
2. Cut a large opening on the handle side of the container.
3. Using the scissor points, fashion two opposing holes on the neck of the container.
4. Make four holes, from the inside out, on the bottom of the container, using the screw.

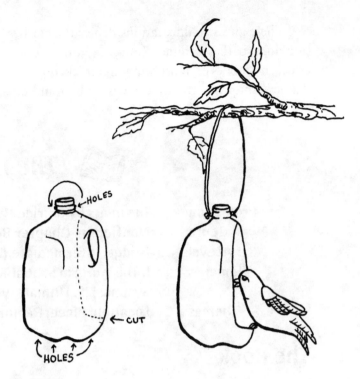

Figure 3.1

5. Working with an adult, determine the length of twine needed to suspend the feeder at an appropriate height. Thread the twine through the holes in the neck and knot the ends.
6. Fill the feeder with seed.
7. Working with an adult, hang the feeder.

Charting with More Books

Mama, Do You Love Me?

Projection:	*Mama, Do You Love Me?* by Barbara M. Joosse, 1991
Genre:	Picture Storybook
Level:	Primary (K–2)
Elements:	I. The World in Spatial Terms; II. Places and Regions
Themes:	Location; Place; Region; Human/Environment Interaction

The Book

This is a story of a mother's love that never wavers for her child. A little Inuit girl asked that most important question, "Mama, do you love me?" while putting her mother's love to a variety of demanding tests. Threatening to live with wolves in a cave and stuffing Mama's mukluks with lemmings were but two. Yet the mother always reassured her that she would always love her little "Dear One."

The expressive illustrations depict the clothes (mukluks, parkas), animals (musk ox, puffin, polar bear), and modes of transportation (umiak, dogsled) that are unique to the Inuit environment and climate. The author also provides a brief description of Inuit history and culture with an accompanying glossary that explains the Inuit terms found in the story.

 # The Inuits

Projection:	*The Inuits* by Shirlee P. Newman, 1993
Genre:	Nonfiction; Chapter Book
Level:	Bridge; Intermediate (2–6)
Elements:	I. The World in Spatial Terms; II. Places and Regions; III. Physical Systems; IV. Human Systems
Themes:	Location; Place; Region; Human/Environment Interaction

The Book

One group of people who live in the Arctic are the Inuits. This book contains information and pictures depicting the lives of past and present Inuits, relating what they do to survive in one of the world's harshest climates. Their homes, fishing and hunting methods, clothing, family and community life, and means of transportation are presented. The Inuit face the challenge of preserving their unique culture in a modern environment for today's children and those of the future.

 # Yuit

Projection:	*Yuit* by Yvette Edmonds, 1993
Genre:	Fiction
Level:	Bridge; Intermediate (2–6)
Elements:	I. The World in Spatial Terms; II. Places and Regions; III. Physical Systems; IV. Human Systems
Themes:	Location; Place; Region; Human/Environment Interaction

The Book

Liak, an Inuit girl, decided to raise an orphaned albino seal pup called Yuit. Since albino seals were considered unlucky, the death of Yuit and her own banishment from the tribe by the medicine man were to be Liak's punishment. Liak and Yuit escaped and traveled through the night to the next settlement for help. The trip, though filled with harrowing experiences, proved successful. Liak stayed at the mission and went to school while Yuit was cared for by a marine biologist.

Immigrants

Projection: *Immigrants* by Martin W. Sandler, 1995
Genre: **Information Book**
Level: **Intermediate (4–6)**
Elements: **I. The World in Spatial Terms; IV. Human Systems; VI. The Uses of Geography**
Themes: **Location; Movement; Human/Environment Interaction**

The Book

A graphic presentation of the immigrants who came to America from Europe from the 1870s to the 1920s is the focus of this book, from the trek across the ocean to the first sight of the Statue of Liberty and the stressful process of passing through Ellis Island. Explicit and sensitive photos and drawings provide the reader with information about where immigrants settled, how they lived and worked, and how they were educated.

The Ox-Cart Man

Projection: *The Ox-Cart Man* by Donald Hall, 1979
Genre: **Picture Storybook**
Level: **Primary (K–2)**
Elements: **I. The World in Spatial Terms; II. Places and Regions; III. Physical Systems; V. Environment and Society**
Themes: **Location; Region; Human/Environment Interaction**

The Book

The seasonal work and life of a farmer and his family in New England are described in this Caldecott Award book. In the fall, the farmer packed his ox-cart with the goods his family made and the produce they grew that year. He traveled to the market, where he sold everything, including his oxen. He bought special gifts for each family member and wintergreen candies for everyone.

The winter work included tapping maple trees for syrup and making maple-sugar candy. With the coming of spring, the family tilled the soil and planted seeds. The cycle continued with the fall harvest.

Realm References

Edmonds, Y. 1993. *Yuit*. Toronto, Canada: Napoleon.

Hall, D. 1979. *The Ox-Cart Man*. New York: Puffin Books.

Hopkins, D. 1995. *Sweet Clara and the Freedom Quilt*. New York: Random House.

Joosse, B. M. 1991. *Mama, Do You Love Me?* San Francisco: Chronicle Books.

Kellogg, S. 1996. *Johnny Appleseed*. New York: William Morrow.

Lerner, C. 1996. *The Backyard Birds of Summer*. New York: Morrow Junior Books.

Newman, S. P. 1993. *The Inuits*. New York: Franklin Watts.

Sandler, M. W. 1995. *Immigrants*. New York: HarperCollins.

Chapter 4
Middle American Realm

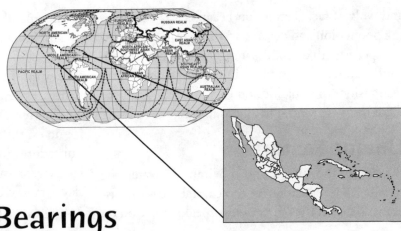

 Getting Your Bearings

Location

This realm consists in part of the funnel-like land-bridge mainland, Mexico, and the seven Central American countries of Guatemala, Belize, Honduras, El Salvador, Nicaragua, Costa Rica, and Panama. The island countries, which include the Greater Antilles—Cuba, Hispaniola, Puerto Rico, and Jamaica—as well as the smaller islands in the Lesser Antilles, make up the rest of the realm. This realm is bordered by the United States on the north and South America on the south and lies between the Atlantic and Pacific Oceans. Middle America is situated between 33°N and 7°N latitude and 59°W and 117°W longitude. The total area of the mainland section is 964,137 square miles. Mexico, the largest country of the realm, also boasts the largest city, its capital, Mexico City, with almost ten million inhabitants.

Topography

The mainland is characterized by mountains, highlands, plateaus, rolling hills, and plains. Mexico is dominated by three mountain ranges (Sierra Madre Occidental, Sierra Madre Oriental, and Sierra Madre del Sur) with dry highlands in between in the north. The two highest peaks in the realm are Citlaltépetl (18,700 feet) and Popocatépetl (17,887 feet) in Mexico. The Yucatán Peninsula and the land adjacent to the Gulf of Mexico are lowlands. In the Central American countries, mountains dominate the landscape, with intermittent lowlands on both coasts. The highest peak in Central America is in Guatemala: Volcán Tajumulco at 13,845 feet. The tropical

islands are mostly lowlands dotted with low mountains. The Rio Grande forms part of the border between Mexico and the United States. In Nicaragua, Lake Nicaragua and Lake Managua are two large bodies of fresh water. Because of its location, the Chagres River in Panama laid the foundation for the Panama Canal.

Climate

An arid and semiarid climate covers over half of Mexico in the north. Along the Gulf Coast more rainfall and tropical conditions exist. In Central America, three climatic zones determined by elevation include the hot country (average exceeds 75°F), temperate country (average temperature of 68° to 74°F), and the cold country (55° to 68°F). Rainfall is seasonal, with most of the 70 inches falling during the summer. The island nations have a primarily tropical climate characterized by hot temperatures and seasonal hurricanes.

Flora and Fauna

Northern Mexico, because of its low rainfall, has cacti, yucca, and mesquite. On the Baja Peninsula, the strangely shaped ciro tree is dispersed throughout the landscape. In the Yucatán, agave, which is used for making rope, is plentiful. At higher elevations, pine and oak trees grow. Dense tropical rain forest covers much of Central America. Coffee, sugarcane, and bananas are grown in both Central America and the island nations of the realm. In Mexico much of the wildlife, such as grizzly bears and wolves, faces extinction because of a burgeoning population and deforestation. Reptiles are commonplace, with crocodiles indigenous to the Central American region. Sea life is important to the entire realm, since the Atlantic and Pacific Oceans and the Caribbean are central to all economies.

Unique Features

Because of the climate and proximity to water, the tourist trade flourishes in the coastal areas and islands. Belize is the only English-speaking nation on the mainland; the other mainland nations use Spanish and Indian languages. English, French, and Spanish are spoken throughout the Caribbean islands. Widespread poverty characterizes this realm. Remnants of the ancient Maya and Aztec cultures, including temples, pyramids, and ball courts, can be found on the mainland. Spanish explorers and conquistadores influenced the entire realm with their language, customs, and the "seeds of change." The slave trade created an interesting mix of races and customs in the Caribbean islands.

Mapping

 Diego

Projection:	*Diego* by Jonah Winter, 1991
Genre:	Biography
Level:	Primary; Bridge (K–4)
Elements:	I. The World in Spatial Terms; II. Places and Regions
Themes:	Location; Region

The Book

The book retells, in simple text and drawings, the life of Mexico's most famous painter, Diego Rivera. Born in Guanajuato in 1886, he became ill and spent his early years regaining his health in the mountains. There he got to know the plants and became friends with the animals. Given a present of colored chalks as a homecoming present, Rivera began to cover the walls with colorful drawings of the things he had seen.

When he was older, he painted murals that told of the history and the lives of his people and the environment in which they lived. Rivera painted the murals in public spaces so that all people could view them. His reputation spread outside Mexico because his paintings brought about a revolution in art.

Key Understandings

Artists can show the people, culture, flora and fauna, and landscapes of a country through their work.

Diego Rivera developed the concept of painting the human and geographic environment of Mexico in mural form.

Knowledge

- Describe the events in the life of Diego Rivera.
- Identify the events in Rivera's life that affected his art.
- Identify the content of Rivera's murals.
- Compare and contrast the content of Rivera's murals to students' human and geographic environments.

Skills

- Ask questions about the people, culture, flora and fauna, and landscapes of Mexico and the students' environment.
- Find information and pictures in trade books.
- Organize the information and pictures of Mexico into a class mural.

- Organize the information and pictures of the students' environment into a class mural.
- Compare and contrast the murals.
- Draw conclusions about the similarities between the two environments.

Perspectives

- Recognize and appreciate the contributions of Diego Rivera to Mexican culture.

Activities

I = Individual　　　P = Pairs　　　G = Group

A. PICTURING RIVERA'S MEXICO (I, P)

Materials: magazines (e.g., *National Geographic World*), trade books, globe, wall map of Middle America and North America, outline map of Mexico, scissors, white glue, crayons

Students, with adult help, should locate Mexico and their own country on the globe and the wall map. Outline and then color in the outline map of Mexico. Using several sources (magazines and books), find pictures of Mexican people and environments and either cut out and glue or draw pictures of them on the outline map.

Questions to Ask

1. What countries are north of Mexico?
2. Which country forms the northern border with Mexico?
3. Looking at the wall map, which country is larger?
4. After tracing and coloring Mexico, what is the shape like?
5. After selecting and organizing the pictures, what plants and animals did you find? What land forms were shown? What work and fun activities are people doing?

B. PAINTING RIVERA'S MEXICO (G)

Materials: roll of butcher paper, poster paint, brushes of various sizes, masking tape, marking pens, pencils

In groups of four or five, students plan the scene of Mexico they are going to paint. The teacher should coordinate the scenes so that there will be a broad spectrum of Mexico depicted. Each group should sketch what it is going to include in the scene, then paint it. Display the various scenes of Mexico painted on the murals.

C. MATCHING MURALS (G)

Materials: clipboard, paper, pencil

In groups of four or five, have students plan the scene of the local people and environments they are going to paint. Teachers and students should proceed as they did in painting Rivera's Mexico.

Have students walk as a group through the mural exhibit, observing and recording as many likenesses as possible between the two environments and cultures. Have each group draw conclusions about the importance of similarities between cultures and share their thoughts with the class.

The Moon Was at a Fiesta

Projection: *The Moon Was at a Fiesta* by Matthew Gollub, 1994
Genre: **Picture Storybook**
Level: Primary; Bridge (K–4)
Elements: **I. The World in Spatial Terms; II. Places and Regions**
Themes: **Location; Place**

The Book

The stars complained to the moon that they could not come out with the sun to see the people of Oaxaca doing fun things while dressed in their colorful clothes. Having slept all day so as to shine at night, the moon was unaware of the people's activity until one day she was awakened by the noise of fireworks. The moon looked down and saw the people having a happy daytime fiesta. She held a special fiesta that night with lanterns for seeing, music for dancing, and tamales and fish soup for eating. The stars twinkled as the moon stayed bright as long as she could for the people's celebration.

When the sun came up the people were sleeping. That day the fields were not plowed and the corn was not ground. The moon realized her mistake and stayed awake at night so the people could sleep, not play. Yet every so often, remembering the all-night fiesta, the moon remains in the sky while the sun rises. When that happens, the people of Oaxaca say that the moon was at a fiesta.

Key Understandings

Cultural celebrations have often been created around the movements of celestial bodies such as the sun, moon, and stars.

Knowledge

- Identify celestial bodies such as the sun, moon, and major stars or star systems.
- State the reasons for the importance of these bodies to the lives of the people of Mexico and students' own lives.
- Determine the times of the year when the moon and the sun may appear together.
- Describe the purpose of the fiesta in Mexican culture.

Skills

- Ask questions about the rising and setting of the sun and the phases of the moon.
- Ask questions about the cultural celebrations called "fiestas."
- Find information in trade books and magazines.
- Compare the sun's movement to that of the moon; draw conclusions from the comparison.
- Connect the time for fiestas to celestial movements.

Perspectives

Cultural celebrations of diverse regions and the reasons for them should be respected.

Activities

I = Individual   P = Pairs   G = Group

A. TRACKING THE DAY AND NIGHT SKY (I)

Materials: clipboard, blank paper, outline map of Mexico, orange and green construction paper, scissors, glue stick, markers, *The Glow-in-the-Dark Night Sky Book* by Clint Hatchett or other similar books with pictures of constellations

First, have students pretend to be birds flying over their own houses or apartments, then draw the aerial view, remembering to include any porches or patios. Students should get up early in the morning to observe on which side of their homes the sun rises, then glue a cutout sun on that side of the aerial drawing. In the evening, students should observe the sunset and place another sun on the corresponding side. At noon on a sunny day, students should stand in their front yards in such a way that their shadows are in front of them. The shadows will point to the north.

The south will be at their backs. The east will be to the right and the west will be to the left. Having determined these directions, have students mark the cardinal directions on their aerial drawings. East should correspond to the rising sun and west to the setting sun. Using an aerial map of the school, have students predict the sunrise and sunset directions, then verify their choices with observations. On an outline map of Mexico, have students draw a compass rose with directions depicted accurately and mark the sunrise and sunset with suns.

Using any night-sky book, parents can help children locate Polaris (the North Star) in the night sky and, if possible, the Big Dipper and the Little Dipper and the moon in various phases throughout the month. Students can then cut out several examples to represent each moon phase. At the top of the aerial map, have students glue the four phases of the moon. Have adults help students label the date on which each phase was observed.

Questions to Ask

1. From what direction does the sun always rise? At what direction does the sun always set?
2. How can you determine north on a sunny day?
3. Can you predict on what side of the school building the sun will rise and set?

Questions to Ask

1. What do the Big and Little Dippers look like?
2. Is the North Star near either the Big or the Little Dipper?
3. How does the moon change throughout the month?
4. Have you ever seen the moon and sun in the sky together?

B. MAKING MOTION MONIGOTES (I)

Materials: **card stock, brads, paint stirrers, crayons, multicolored ribbons or knitting yarn, scissors, white glue, monigotes, reproducibles, one-hole punch, stapler, CD of authentic Mexican music and CD player**

Moving the monigotes to music.

Make copies of the reproducible on card stock (see Figures 4.1 and 4.2 on pages 44 and 45). Have students cut these out. Punch a hole through each of the small circles drawn on the parts of the figures. Using the brads, connect corresponding numbers to make the male or female figure. Color in clothes for both figures; cut equal lengths of ribbon or yarn and glue them to the waistline of the female figure to decorate the skirt. Draw in the children's faces. Staple the pantilla and sombrero to their own paint stirrer, attaching them with brads to the backs of the figures. With an authentic Mexican tune playing in the background and while holding the wooden paint stirrers, have students practice moving their monigotes to the music.

c. SUN FUN FIESTA (G)

Materials: **CD of authentic Mexican music and CD player, motion monigotes, tamales, filling for tamales, nachos, salsa, guacamole, books about games and dances**

Have each group act as padrinos to plan and hold a daytime fiesta celebrating the sun. Padrinos (godparents) plan the food, games, and the music for the motion monigotes. Enlist the help of parents and older children to coordinate efforts on the day of the fiesta.

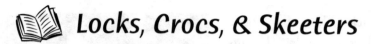

Locks, Crocs, & Skeeters

Projection: *Locks, Crocs, & Skeeters* by Nancy Winslow Parker, 1996
Genre: **Information Book**
Level: **Intermediate (4–6)**
Elements: **I. The World in Spatial Terms; II. Places and Regions; III. Physical Systems; V. Environment and Society**
Themes: **Location; Place; Movement**

The Book

This two-part book begins with a poem written in 1906 by James Stanley Gilbert titled "Beyond the Chagres." Illustrated by the author, the rhyming text of the first part tells of the dangers that await the traveler in this tropical region. Crocodiles, scorpions, boa constrictors, cougars, and "perils of a million different breeds" abound in the area surrounding the Chagres River, located on the Isthmus of Panama.

The second part tells the story of the building of the Panama Canal across the isthmus. Under the direction of a French engineer, Ferdinand-Marie de Lesseps, construction began in the mosquito-infested jungle in 1881. The French effort failed, and the United States signed a treaty with the new Panamanian government to build the canal. For ten years (1904 to 1914), at a cost of almost $400 million and over 4,000 deaths, the United States completed this 50-mile-long, lock-engineered, human-made wonder of the world.

Key Understandings

Throughout time people have modified the natural landscape to meet their physical and economic needs. The building of the Panama Canal across the Isthmus of Panama created a shorter and faster connection for trade and transportation between the Atlantic and Pacific Oceans.

Knowledge

- Identify the location and environment of the Isthmus of Panama.

- Identify the early explorers who first searched the area for a passage between the Atlantic and Pacific Oceans.
- Describe the construction of the Panama Canal from the points of view of French and U.S. involvement.
- Recount the environmental dangers that were faced by the builders of the canal.
- Describe a voyage through the canal.
- Evaluate the canal's significance in the past, present, and future.

Skills

- Ask questions about the location of Panama and the canal.
- Ask questions about the construction and operation of the canal.
- Obtain information from reference books, maps, and globes.
- Arrange the information in sequence according to the events of the past and present.
- Interpret the data to make predictions about the future of the isthmus and the canal.

Perspectives

Appreciate the historical significance of the building and operation of the Panama Canal.

Activities

I = Individual   P = Pairs   G = Group

A. Voyaging the Canal (I)

Materials: student atlas, globe, wall map, Panama Canal map (*Locks, Crocs, & Skeeters*, pp. 26–27), outline map of Middle America, crayons or colored pencils, markers

Locate Middle America on the wall map and globe. On the outline map, label and color the major bodies of water, land forms, and countries. Create a legend noting rain forest, mountains, rivers, flat lands, and so on. If the map does not have a distance scale, have students develop one. Use the map of the Panama Canal to determine the route.

Questions to Ask

1. What is the relative location of Panama?
2. What environmental and physical barriers did the builders of the Panama Canal face?
3. What is the width of the Isthmus of Panama at its narrowest point?
4. How long is the canal from the Atlantic to the Pacific?
5. How many canal locks are there from end to end?

B. The Canal Game (1904–1914) (P)

Materials: large pizza box, clear contact paper, marking pens, poster paint, brushes, miniature plastic boats, dice, colored 3 x 5-inch cards, white glue, small Ziploc-type bag, rubber bands

On the top and bottom of the inside of the pizza box, draw the Panama Canal, including all locks and land and water forms (*Locks, Crocs, & Skeeters*, pp. 26–27). Paint it with the appropriate colors. Block and number the playing field (canal route). On one of the cards, write the directions for play and glue them to the board surface. Develop a list of historical questions with answers concerning the building of the canal. In addition, develop a list of statements concerning environmental and physical barriers. Record the questions and statements on individual 3 x 5-inch cards. Record the answers on the reverse sides of the question cards. Have players roll the dice to move forward. Barrier cards must state the number of spaces that the players drawing them should move backward. The winner is the one who advances through the canal first. Cover the game board with clear contact paper to protect it. Laminate the game cards and store them wrapped in a rubber band. Place the game pieces and dice in the plastic bag.

Figure 4.1–Motion Monigote (Female)

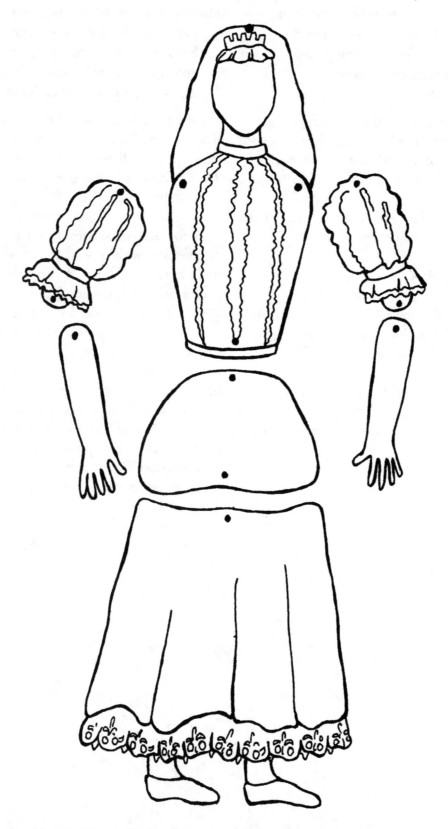

Figure 4.2–Motion Monigote (Male)

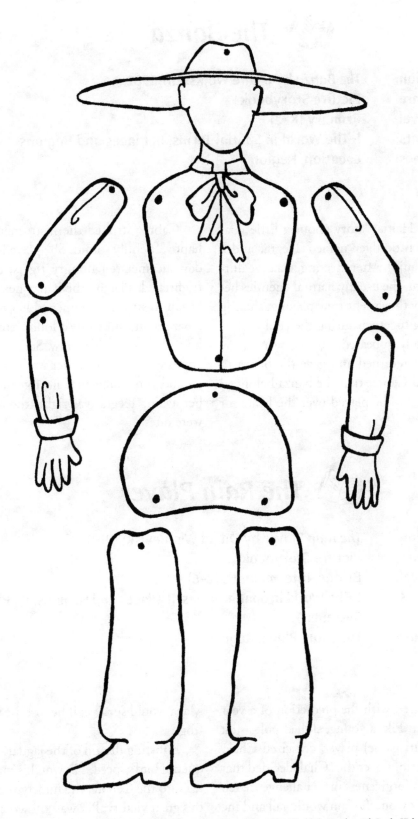

Charting with More Books

 ## The Banza

Projection: *The Banza* by Diane Wolkstein, 1981
Genre: Picture Storybook
Level: Primary (K-2)
Elements: I. The World in Spatial Terms; II. Places and Regions
Themes: Location; Region

The Book

This book tells a Haitian story about a little goat named Cabree, a little tiger named Teegra, and a beautiful banza (banjo). After meeting in a cave during a thunderstorm, the usually natural enemies became friends. They then spent time playing, sharing food, and sleeping together during the cool nights. Soon Teegra's family appeared, and he went away with them. Teegra returned and gave the banza to his friend. He told Cabree that the banza belonged to the heart; it was to be played over the heart for protection.

Cabree stroked the instrument, and it made a happy, friendly sound. She played many tunes. One day she met ten hungry tigers, and she was very frightened. Placing the banza next to her heart, she began to strum. She opened her mouth and, to her amazement, out came a loud, ferocious song about how Cabree ate tigers raw. Suddenly nine tigers disappeared and their leader was left, begging to be let go and promising that no tiger would ever bother her again. Teegra was right; the banza and Cabree were one.

 ## The Rain Player

Projection: *The Rain Player* by David Wisniewski, 1991
Genre: Picture Storybook
Level: Bridge; Intermediate (2-6)
Elements: I. The World in Spatial Terms; II. Places and Regions; III. Physical Systems
Themes: Location; Place; Region

The Book

The Maya were faced with the prediction of a year of terrible drought. Pik, a young, skilled pok-a-tok (a rubber-ball court game) player, criticized Chak, the god of rain. Furious over this, Chak decided that Pik should win his forgiveness in a challenge match of pok-a-tok. If Pik won, the rain would fall and the Maya would survive; if he lost, he would turn into a frog.

Enlisting the aid of the jaguar's strength, and the quetzal bird's speed, Pik won his matches when Chak fell into the Cenote, the underground pit. Because of this great victory, Pik was known as the Rain Player.

Pyramid of the Sun, Pyramid of the Moon

Projection:	*Pyramid of the Sun, Pyramid of the Moon* by Leonard E. Fisher, 1988
Genre:	**Information Book**
Level:	**Intermediate (4–6)**
Elements:	**I. The World in Spatial Terms; II. Places and Regions; V. Environment and Society**
Themes:	**Location; Place**

The Book

Around A.D. 100, the Toltec Indians built two great pyramids in the sacred city of Teotihuacán in the Valley of Mexico. Nearly 200 feet high, the larger of the two was the Pyramid of the Sun, which was connected by the long Avenue of the Dead to the Pyramid of the Moon. Religious ceremonies worshipping the sun, wind, stars, jaguars, and serpents were held there. A series of catastrophes forced the Toltecs to abandon Teotihuacán.

When the Aztecs came to power in 1400, they believed that the gods still resided there. They would return to the two pyramids for special rites and make human sacrifices to the gods. There it was foretold to Montezuma II that the light-skinned, "feathered spirit" would return and reclaim the land.

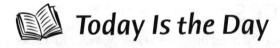 # Today Is the Day

Projection:	*Today Is the Day* by Nancy Rieken, 1996
Genre:	**Picture Storybook**
Level:	**Bridge (2–4)**
Elements:	**I. The World in Spatial Terms; II. Places and Regions; III. Physical Systems; IV. Human Systems**
Themes:	**Location; Place; Movement**

The Book

Yese, a young Mexican girl, her older sister, Yara, and her baby brother, Juanito, awoke to a very special day; with their mother, they awaited the return of their father, who had been away for six months. Since there had been no rain for a long time, the corn crop hadn't grown and there was no money for the family, not even enough to buy shoes so the girls could go to school, so their father had been forced to look for work in a place far away.

Yese went to the road to meet the bus, but her father was not on any of them. The family waited together by the road at night for the last bus. The unhappy group watched while the bus passed by. As they were about to return to the house, a car stopped, and out came Yese's papa. He was not rich, but Yese didn't care, for her father was more important than money.

📖 A Family in Jamaica

Projection:	*A Family in Jamaica* by John and Penny Hubley, 1985
Genre:	Information Book
Level:	Intermediate (4–6)
Elements:	I. The World in Spatial Terms; II. Places and Regions; III. Physical Systems; IV. Human Systems
Themes:	Location; Place; Region; Human/Environment Interaction

The Book

With pictures and text, the book provides a look at the life of the Samuels family in a village in Jamaica through the eyes of ten-year-old Dorothy, who attended the village school and hoped to go to the high school at Montego Bay.

The family lived on a farm and grew vegetables to eat, barter, or sell. Dorothy was lucky because her family raised cows and she always had fresh milk. Every Saturday she went by bus with her mother to Montego Bay to sell their produce at the market. Dorothy liked to see the big shops and the tourists who came to Jamaica for the sunshine and the beaches.

The text includes a brief history of Jamaica from the time of Columbus to its nation status in 1962. The production of Jamaica's most famous crop and leading export, sugar, is shown from planting to refinement.

Realm References

Fisher, L. E. 1988. *Pyramid of the Sun, Pyramid of the Moon.* New York: Macmillan.

Gollub, M. 1994. *The Moon Was at a Fiesta.* New York: Tambourine Books.

Hatchett, C. 1988. *The Glow-in-the-Dark Night Sky Book.* New York: Random House.

Hubley, J., and P. Hubley. 1985. *A Family in Jamaica.* Minneapolis, MN: Lerner Publications.

Parker, N. W. 1996. *Locks, Crocs,& Skeeters.* New York: Greenwillow.

Riecken, N. 1996. *Today Is the Day.* Boston, MA: Houghton Mifflin Children's Books.

Winter, J. 1991. *Diego.* New York: Alfred A. Knopf.

Wisniewski, D. 1991. *The Rain Player.* New York: Clarion Books.

Wolkstein, D. 1981. *The Banza.* New York: Dial Books for Young Readers.

Chapter 5
South American Realm

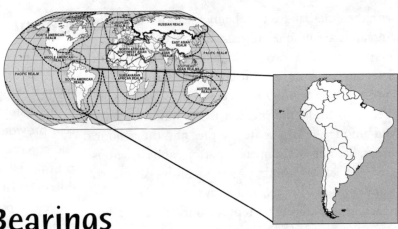

 Getting Your Bearings

Location

South America, the southern continent of the Western Hemisphere, consists of thirteen independent countries: Argentina, Bolivia, Brazil, Chile, Colombia, Ecuador, French Guiana, Guyana, Paraguay, Peru, Suriname, Uruguay, and Venezuela. There are also a number of islands, the most notable of which are the Galápagos Islands in the Pacific, Aruba in the Caribbean, and the Falkland Islands in the Atlantic. This triangular continent lies between the Pacific and Atlantic Oceans and is connected to Middle America on the north where Colombia borders Panama. South America is situated between approximately 12°N and 54°S latitude and 83°W and 35°W longitude. The equator traverses Brazil and Ecuador. South America is the fourth-largest continent, with an area of 6,884,000 square miles. Brazil, the largest country of the realm, also has the most populous city, São Paulo, with over twenty-one million people.

Topography

The Andes Mountains, the highest mountains in the Western Hemisphere; the Amazon Basin, the world's largest forest area; and the Amazon River, the longest navigable river, are outstanding features of the continent. Plateaus dominate the rest of South America. Aconcagua Mountain in Argentina is the tallest peak in the Western Hemisphere at 22,834 feet. Shared by Bolivia and Peru, Lake Titicaca is the highest lake in the world. Argentina and Uruguay share a grassy plain called the Pampas.

Climate

South America includes three climate types: temperate, mountain, and tropical. The tropics cover most of South America, yet agents of change such as the mountains and Humboldt and Brazilian currents temper the climate so that temperatures range from 50°F in winter in the Argentine Pampas to 80°F year-round in the Amazon Basin. Generally there are no great extremes of temperature in South America, but wide extremes in rainfall exist. Rain-forest conditions characterize the world's largest tropical wet region, the Amazon Basin, while the Atacama Desert in Chile is the earth's driest place.

Flora and Fauna

Three major divisions of vegetation grow in South America: forest, grassland, and desert. The forests include the tropical rain forest, evergreens, palm forest, and tropical deciduous forest. Products from the forest areas include chocolate, rubber, cashews, Brazil nuts, and quinine. Within the wooded lands of the deciduous forests cacti and other thorny, spiny plants grow in what is called the thorn forest. The rich grasslands, the Pampas, are the basis of Argentina's agricultural economy. Cacti, desert scrub, and cushion plants populate the desert regions.

Llamas and alpacas are of economic importance for their wool. Other unusual species include tapirs, peccaries, jaguars, mountain lions, cougars, ocelots, monkeys (the capuchin, ring-tailed, is the most abundant monkey in South America), and marmosets. Bats are numerous. This realm is home to the armadillo, with the nine-banded type being the most common. Anteaters are unique animals, the largest being the ant bear, standing two feet high with a two-foot tail. Seals and sea lions inhabit both the Pacific and Atlantic coasts. South America abounds with many species of birds; the smallest is the hummingbird, and among the largest are the rhea and the condor. Ibises, flamingos, trumpeters, parrots, and cockatoos are other exotic South American birds. Alligators, giant tortoises, lizards, and such large snakes as the anaconda are among the reptiles found in this realm.

Unique Features

Angel Falls, on a tributary of the Orinoco River in Venezuela, is the tallest waterfall in the world. The interior of this poor but richly resource-endowed realm is largely uninhabited. The Amazon rain-forest ecosystem provides the earth with a fifth of its fresh water and covers an area that is only a little smaller than the continental United States. Although Spanish is the dominant language of the South American realm, Portuguese is spoken in the largest country, Brazil. In addition, several Indian languages, such as Quechua and Aymara, are still spoken in Bolivia, Peru, and Ecuador.

 # Mapping

 ## Tonight Is Carnaval

Projection:	*Tonight Is Carnaval* by Arthur Dorros, 1991
Genre:	Picture Storybook
Level:	Primary; Bridge (K–4)
Elements:	I. The World in Spatial Terms; II. Places and Regions; III. Physical Systems; IV. Human Systems
Themes:	Location; Place

The Book

Every year the Peruvians celebrate for three days and nights before Lent with a carnaval. The people sing and dance to the playing of bands, with many hiding their faces behind masks. There is great merriment. The story is told by a young boy who played the *quena* flute in his father's band and who eagerly counted the days to carnaval. Photographs of *arpilleras,* the native wall hangings, colorfully illustrate the family at work and play before the celebration.

The boy's whole family had many tasks to do before the carnaval. The fields needed plowing and planting. The llamas had to be taken into the high mountains to feed on the grass, and the potatoes had to be harvested. Finally everything was done, and the family boarded the truck to go to carnaval. The young boy happily played his flute while the people sang and danced to the music.

Key Understandings

Throughout time people have developed ceremonies that demonstrate their beliefs: *Carnaval* is an example of such a tradition. The geography of the region often influences the unique preparations and activities that are a part of this celebration.

Knowledge

- Describe the activities the family had to complete to prepare for carnaval.
- Identify the role of flora and fauna in the preparations.
- Identify the musical instruments that are played at carnaval.
- Compare and contrast preparation and celebration for carnaval to a national holiday in the United States such as Thanksgiving.

Skills

- Ask questions about the mountain habitat of the Andes and the Peruvian family in the book.
- Ask questions about the activities that help the family prepare for carnaval.
- Find information and pictures about Peru in magazines, atlases, and trade books.
- Organize the information into a group wall hanging (arpilleras) for display.
- Categorize the information from the various wall hangings under leisure tasks and work tasks.
- Compare carnaval to Thanksgiving and draw conclusions.

Perspectives

Recognize the importance of celebrations in our lives.

Activities

I = Individual   P = Pairs   G = Group

A. PINPOINTING PERU (I, G)

Materials: globe, wall map of South America, travel magazines, trade books, children's atlas, file folders

Locate Peru on the globe, children's atlas, and wall map. Describe its relative location to the United States. Have the children note the Andes Mountains in the pictures in the book. Look for pictures of Peru and the Andes in the travel magazines and trade books, especially noticing the llamas. Collect and categorize the pictures by placing them in leisure and work task file folders.

Questions to Ask

1. Where is Peru located?
2. Is the United States north or south of Peru?
3. Are there mountains in Peru and the United States?
4. What types of animals and plants do you find in Peru?
5. What work and play activity pictures did you find and categorize?

B. ARPILLERAS ART (G)

Materials: felt squares in a variety of colors, colorful yarns, cottonballs, white glue, scissors

The teacher should discuss with the students the necessary components and their placement. For example, in the mountain scenes the mountains are always in the background, as are the sun and the clouds. Using the pictures in the book as a guide, determine a particular scene to illustrate. Each student makes a mental map of the arpillera that would best illustrate the selected scene. As a group, discuss individual mental maps in order to select the best components for the group project. On a piece of drawing paper, the students should plan the scene. Next, the group determines who will be responsible for the various objects that will be components of the arpilleras. Draw the outlines for the figures on the felt. Cut out the components and collaborate on gluing them in place. (Some teacher assistance may be required for cutting felt.) Add yarn and cotton where appropriate. When complete, display the arpilleras around the room. Students will view the arpilleras and take note of the flora and fauna and various activities pictured. In the groups, students will list all of the features they saw in the arpilleras.

Sewing a scene.

c. COMPARING CELEBRATIONS (G)

Materials: list of features, pencil, paper

In each group students will discuss and list the preparations and celebration for Thanksgiving. Compare in a group discussion based on the two lists the similarities and differences that both cultures experience in the two celebrations (carnaval and Thanksgiving). Report the findings to the class. Finally, choose the best parts of carnaval and Thanksgiving. Students must provide evidence for their choices.

My Mama's Little Ranch on the Pampas

Projection:	*My Mama's Little Ranch on the Pampas* by Maria Christina Brusca, 1994
Genre:	Picture Storybook
Level:	Bridge (2–4)
Elements:	I. The World in Spatial Terms; II. Places and Regions; III. Physical Systems; V. Environment and Society
Themes:	Location; Place; Region; Human/Environment Interaction

The Book

A child's life on a small ranch on the Pampas in Argentina is the highlight of the book. The author, Maria, recalled her adventures on school holidays with her brother on the lush green plains of the Pampas. Maria had daily chores, such as feeding pigs and milking cows. Most of all, Maria liked to care for the cows and young calves. Riding her horse like the *gauchos*, she spent her time herding the cows for branding and caring for the calves during the rainy season. Her free time was spent braiding harnesses, listening to gaucho stories, and riding the range hunting for *peludos* while attempting to avoid contact with *la luz mala*. In addition, she drove the sulky into town, where she and her brother danced the heel-toe-stomping *malambo*.

Key Understandings

The climate and topography of the Pampas determine the economics and lifestyle of the people. A unique culture has developed as a result of ranching in this region.

Knowledge

- Relate the activities that are necessary for life on Maria's ranch on the Pampas.
- Describe how the climate of the Pampas affects activities on the ranch.
- Articulate the characteristics, culture, and habitat of the gaucho.
- Compare and contrast the gaucho with the U.S. cowboy.

Skills

- Ask questions about the location, topography, and climate of the Pampas.
- Ask questions about the flora and fauna of the Pampas.
- Ask questions about the people who live and work on the Pampas.
- Find information and pictures about the life and work of the gauchos in Argentina and Uruguay.
- Find information and pictures about the U.S. cowboy.
- Organize and categorize the information into a web for each one.
- Compare gauchos to cowboys and draw conclusions.

Perspectives

Respect the ways that people make a living on a ranch on the Pampas.

Activities

I = Individual   P = Pairs   G = Group

A. PAMPAS LATITUDES (I)

Materials: atlas, geography reference books, endpapers of the book, globe, wall map of the Western Hemisphere and South America, outline map of the Western Hemisphere, pencils, markers, crayons, ruler

Using the globe and the wall map, find the Western Hemisphere, noting the continents and three realms. In addition, locate the equator at 0° latitude, the Tropic of Cancer at 23.5°N latitude, the Tropic of Capricorn at 23.5°S latitude, the Arctic Circle, and the Antarctic Circle. On the map of South America, locate the latitudes for the Pampas. On the outline map, beginning at the equator, draw and label with appropriate degrees the lines of latitude for every 20° north and south. Draw and label the equator, the Tropics of Cancer and Capricorn, and the Arctic and Antarctic Circles. Using the lines of latitude as a reference, color and label the Pampas.

Questions to Ask

1. Between which lines of latitude on your map is the Pampas located? Is the Pampas north or south of the equator?
2. How close in degrees is the Pampas to the Tropic of Capricorn?
3. Considering the direct rays of the sun, what is the relationship of the Tropics of Cancer and Capricorn to the seasons? How does the location north or south of the equator impact the seasons?
4. When it is winter at your location, what season is it on the Pampas? Why do you think this difference occurs?

B. PERSONAL PAMPAS STORIES (I)

Materials: *National Geographic* and *Geographic World* and travel magazines, trade books, encyclopedia, writing paper, pencils, crayons

Using the magazines, encyclopedia, and trade books, students should gather data about the lives of children growing up on a ranch on the Pampas. Students imagine what life would be like living on a ranch. Develop short stories concerning the work and play that they would be engaged in if they lived on the Pampas. This should include the types of animals, an encounter with *la luz mala*, and the effects of climate and terrain. Each student will illustrate, share, and display the Pampas stories.

C. COWBOYS AND GAUCHOS (P)

Materials: Venn diagram reproducible, *National Geographic* and *Geographic World*, trade books on gauchos and cowboys, encyclopedia, poster board, colored markers, white glue, scissors

Search for information and pictures about the work, clothing, habitat, and lifestyle of the gaucho and the U.S. cowboy. Organize the information into three categories: (1) gaucho, (2) cowboy, and (3) shared characteristics. Using the reproducible Venn diagram (see Figure 5.1 on page 56), list the items in the appropriate sections, remembering to use the section where the circles intersect for shared characteristics. Transfer information to the poster board using the diagram as the data framework. Add pictures, drawings, and a title to the poster. In a presentation, one partner will explain information about the U.S. cowboy and the other about the gaucho. Conclusions should be formulated about similarities and differences. Display completed posters.

Amazon: A Young Reader's Look at the Last Frontier

Projection:	*Amazon: A Young Reader's Look at the Last Frontier* by Peter Lourie, 1991
Genre:	**Information Book; Chapter Book**
Level:	**Intermediate (4-6)**
Elements:	**I. The World in Spatial Terms; II. Places and Regions; III. Physical Systems; IV. Human Systems; V. Environment and Society; VI. The Uses of Geography**
Themes:	**Location; Place; Region**

The Book

Civilization is making disastrous headway in destroying the Amazon rain forest, the last frontier. Not only is this destruction ruining the traditional lifestyle of the natives who survive on the river and the forest that lines its shores, but the result of the cutting down and burning of trees to make way for settlements in the Amazon Basin also has had an impact on global warming, the "greenhouse effect."

The book takes the reader on a journey through the heart of the Amazon in the Brazilian state of Rondônia. Through the descriptive text and the colorful photographs, the reader is provided with a view of the way the natives work and play in this habitat. The results of the devastation to people, flora, and fauna are clearly evident.

Key Understandings

The encroachment of human civilization on the rain forest will impact future environmental conditions on Earth.

Knowledge

- Describe the ecosystem of the Amazon rain forest.
- Explain global warming and the greenhouse effect in relation to the destruction of the rain forest.
- Identify the various ways that people are destroying the rain forest.

- Predict the effects of a diminished rain forest on future generations of people.

Skills

- Ask questions about the characteristics of the Amazon rain forest and the connections to the ecosystem of the region.
- Acquire information concerning the elements of the rain-forest ecosystem.
- Organize and analyze the rain-forest information into three categories: understory, canopy, and emergents.
- Evaluate the impact of human modification of the Amazon ecosystem.

Perspectives

Ecological connections between people and the rain forest must be valued to ensure the future harmony of ecosystems, life forms, and society.

Activities

I = Individual   P = Pairs   G = Group

A. MAPPING THE AMAZON RAIN FOREST

Materials: globe, outline map of the world, student atlas, geography reference books, tracing paper, colored pencils

Using the globe and student atlas, discover the rain forests of the world. On the outline map of the world, color the rain forests green and locate and label the equator. Label the locations of the rain forests around the world. Trace and label the continent and countries of South America, the Amazon Basin (the Amazon River and tributaries), and the Amazon rain forest.

Questions to Ask

1. Using the outline map of the world, what is similar in the relative location of all the rain-forest areas?
2. Which rain-forest area appears to be the largest?
3. In which countries of South America do you find the Amazon rain forest? How many countries are affected by the rain forest?
4. What rivers run through the rain forest? Which one is the largest?
5. Why do you think this area is called the Amazon Basin?

B. THE STAIRWELL RAIN FOREST (G)

Materials: books on the rain forest (encyclopedia, National Geographic, geography books), tissue paper, construction paper, poster paints, butcher paper, branches and twigs, markers, white glue, tape, stapler, rope, twine, feathers, stones, spray bottle with water, humidifier, tape or CD of rain-forest sounds, tape or CD player, and any other appropriate materials (be creative)

The teacher should divide the class into three groups: (1) understory, (2) canopy, and (3) emergents. Each group must find information about the flora and fauna of its assigned level of the rain forest. Select an area in the school building, preferably a stairwell, that would be appropriate for the construction of a three-dimensional rain-forest model. Students should collaborate on placement of rain-forest features on the stairwell to best exemplify the three connecting layers. Design, in draft form, the flora and fauna elements and their placement on paper. In the classroom each group constructs and paints the assigned layer, using creative ideas. Transfer the constructed layers to the stairwell and attach to the wall and railings. Group members take turns acting as stagehands to run the "humidity," "rain," and sounds. Finally, each group should identify a tour director to guide other children on a trip through the stairwell rain forest.

C. ECOSYSTEM JUNGLE JARS (G)

Materials: large glass jars (e.g., mayonnaise jars from the cafeteria), soil, pebbles, tropical plants (houseplants), Inside the Amazing Amazon by Don Lessem, water, earthworms, pails, trowels, jungle journal

With three to four students in each group, provide one glass jar, potting soil, pail, trowel, and houseplants (refer to reference books for names) for each group. Have students in each group gather the additional materials from home when possible. Assemble the mini-ecosystem elements in the jars and cover. Place in a sunlit area. Students observe and record the interaction and continuous recycling of nutrients, water, and air in their jungle journals. Have students determine how their jar ecosystems are like the rain forest. Write a brief description of how their ecosystems would change if the plants were burned like the Amazon rain forest is being burned. Describe the connection to global warming.

Figure 5.1–Venn Diagram

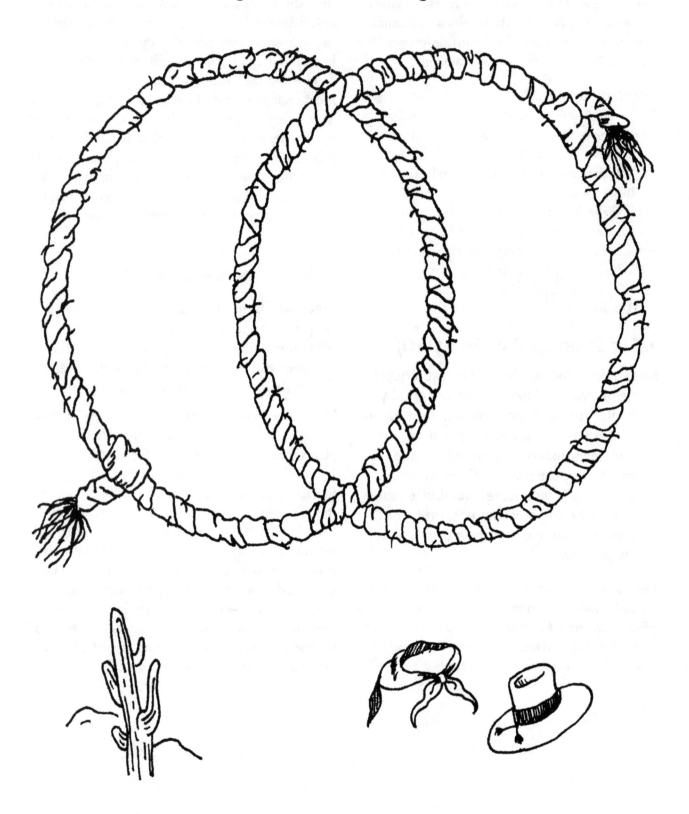

Charting with More Books

 ## Moon Rope: A Peruvian Folktale

Projection:	*Moon Rope: A Peruvian Folktale* retold by Lois Ehlert, 1992
Genre:	Picture Storybook
Level:	Primary (K–2)
Elements:	I. The World in Spatial Terms; II. Places and Regions; III. Physical Systems
Themes:	Location; Place; Region

The Book

The tale relates the adventure of a fox and his friend, the mole. The fox wanted to go to the moon and persuaded the mole to go with him. Fox's plan was to braid grass into a long rope and throw it up high to hook onto the crescent moon. He needed the help of the birds, however, to connect the rope to the moon. As the two were climbing toward their goal, the mole ignored the fox's warning not to look down. He looked, slipped, and fell back to earth. Humiliated by his failure, to this day the mole comes out only at night to avoid all creatures. The birds say that when there is a clear night, they can see the fox looking down from the moon.

 ## Feathers Like a Rainbow: An Amazon Indian Tale

Projection:	*Feathers Like a Rainbow: An Amazon Indian Tale* by Flora, 1989
Genre:	Picture Storybook
Level:	Primary (K–2)
Elements:	I. The World in Spatial Terms; II. Places and Regions
Themes:	Location; Place

The Book

A very long time ago, the birds of the great rain forest had dark feathers. A gray-winged trumpeter, Jacamin, wanted feathers as beautiful as the rainbow. With his mother, he traveled through the forest meeting other birds, such as the macaw and cock-of-the-rock, who also wanted colorful feathers.

They met a tiny, beautifully colored hummingbird who told them that its colors came from the flowers. A drop of rainbow colors would be placed in a bowl, and later the hummingbird would splash the color on its feathers. Greedily, the big birds swooped down, stole the bowl, and used all the colors except one. Jacamin rubbed the remaining color on his breast; that is why the gay-winged trumpeter has a purple breast and an ash-gray back. All the other birds still carry the colors taken from the hummingbird.

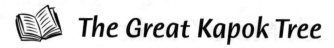

The Great Kapok Tree

Projection:	*The Great Kapok Tree* by Lynne Cherry, 1990
Genre:	Picture Storybook
Level:	Bridge; Intermediate (2–6)
Elements:	I. The World in Spatial Terms; II. Places and Regions; III. Physical Systems; V. Environment and Society
Themes:	Place; Region; Human/Environment Interaction

The Book

The animals who lived in the great Kapok tree watched as a forester began to chop down the tree. Overcome by the work and the intense heat, he fell asleep. The tree fauna—the boa constrictor, bee, monkey, bird, frog, tree porcupine, anteater, and sloth—each whispered a warning in the man's ear about what would happen to them and to people should he chop down the Kapok. An Indian child who lived in the forest whispered a plea to view the fauna and flora inhabitants of the jungle world with new eyes. When he awoke and saw the fauna staring at him and smelled the fragrance of the jungle flora, the man dropped his ax and left.

The Llama's Secret

Projection:	*The Llama's Secret* retold by Argentina Palacios, 1993
Genre:	Legend
Level:	Bridge (2–4)
Elements:	I. The World in Spatial Terms; II. Places and Regions; V. Environment and Society
Themes:	Place; Region; Human/Environment Interaction

The Book

A farmer was worried because his prized possession, the llama, was not eating the meadow grass. One day the llama began to moan and cry. To the farmer's amazement, the llama began to speak. He told the man that *Mamacocha*, the sea, was to flood the earth. If the man would take his family and go to *Huillcacoto*, the highest peak in the mountains, they could be saved. On their way to the mountain they warned other creatures, who followed them in their rush to safety as the waters rose. Having reached their goal, they were frightened because the sun disappeared and it became very cold. The llama foretold that the sun would shine again and that they would be able to descend the mountain. The Peruvians, to this day, show their gratitude by adorning their llamas with little bells and ribbons.

Journey of the Red-Eyed Tree Frog

Projection: *Journey of the Red-Eyed Tree Frog* by Martin and Tanis Jordan, 1992
Genre: Picture StoryBook
Level: Bridge (2–4)
Elements: II. Places and Regions; III. Physical Systems; V. Environment and Society; VI. The Uses of Geography
Themes: Place; Region; Human/Environment Interaction

The Book

This beautifully illustrated book relates the story of two tiny red-eyed tree frogs, Hops-a-Bit and Jumps-a-Little, in their quest to find a solution to the problem of humans burning their forest. Hops-a-Bit journeyed from their island home in Central America to the Amazon Jungle to meet with the Great Wise Frog to find the answer for Jumps-a-Little and himself. Hops-a-Bit met many native animals and viewed the encroachment of humans upon their habitat. The authors include vibrant descriptions of the landscape along the way. The Great Wise Frog told Hops-a-Bit that his island had been saved by concerned people and it was safe for him to return. In addition, he renamed the little red-eyed tree frog Hops-a-Lot because of the long journey he had made in his search for an answer to the problem of the destruction of the rain forests.

Realm References

Brusca, M. C. 1994. *My Mama's Little Ranch on the Pampas*. New York: Henry Holt.

Cherry, L. 1990. *The Great Kapok Tree*. San Diego: Harcourt Brace Jovanovich.

Dorros, A. 1991. *Tonight Is Carnaval*. New York: Dutton Children's Books.

Ehlert, L. 1992. *Moon Rope: A Peruvian Folktale*. San Diego, CA: Harcourt Brace Jovanovich.

Flora. 1989. *Feathers Like a Rainbow: An Amazon Indian Tale*. New York: HarperCollins Children's Books.

Jordan, M., and T. Jordan. 1992. *Journey of the Red-Eyed Tree Frog*. New York: Simon & Schuster.

Lessem, D. 1995. *Inside the Amazing Amazon*. New York: Crown.

Lourie, P. 1991. *Amazon: A Young Reader's Look at the Last Frontier*. Honesdale, PA: Caroline House.

Palacios, A. 1993. *The Llama's Secret*. Mahwah, New Jersey: Troll Associates.

Chapter 6
North African/Southwest Asian Realm

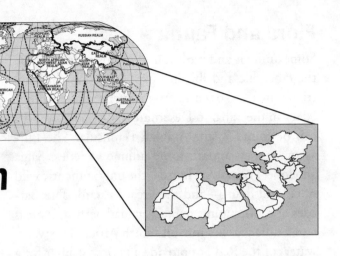

 ## Getting Your Bearings

Location

The North African/Southwest Asian realm consists of a vast array of nations extending from the Atlantic Ocean on the west to China and Pakistan on the east. The Mediterranean Sea, Black Sea, and Russia form a border on the north and the Arabian Sea and High Africa form the border to the south. In North Africa the countries are Mauritania, Morocco, Algeria, Mali, Tunisia, Libya, Niger, Chad, Egypt, and the northern part of Sudan. The countries of Southwest Asia are Israel, Jordan, Saudi Arabia, Yemen, Lebanon, Syria, Turkey, Iraq, United Arab Emirates, Kuwait, Oman, Qatar, Bahrain, Iran, Armenia, Georgia, Azerbaijan, Kazakhstan, Turkmenistan, Uzbekistan, Kyrgyzstan, Tajikistan, and Afghanistan. The five major and most populous cities in descending order are Cairo, Istanbul, Tehran, Baghdad, and Algiers. Istanbul is the only city on earth that straddles two continents: Europe and Asia.

Topography

The Sahara Desert dominates North Africa. The ever-expanding Sahara is the largest desert in the world, with huge sand seas created from weathering and erosion. In the north, arid grasslands called the *sahel* rim the desert. Wadis, or intermittent streams, provide limited water sources for desert travelers. Bordering the desert, the Atlas Mountains stretch from southwest Morocco to northeast Tunisia. The highest mountain in this range is Mount Toubkal at

13,665 feet. The Nile River, the longest river in the world at 4,160 miles, forms an arc-shaped delta that measures 100 miles north to south and 150 miles along the Mediterranean. Southwest Asia is also an area of arid land. In the region known as Turkestan are two deserts, Kara Kum and Kyzyl Kum, and the Pamirs and Tian Shan mountain ranges. The Tigris and Euphrates Rivers join in Iraq, forming reed marshes, one of the few wetland areas of this realm; otherwise Iraq is largely lowland desert. The Elburz Mountains in northern Iran sport the highest peak, Damávand, at 18,934 feet. In Israel in the Middle East region, the salty Dead Sea is the lowest point on the earth's surface, about 1,312 feet below sea level. Turkey is largely mountainous, with the Pontic Mountains and several other ranges in the north and the Taurus Mountains and other ranges in the south, surrounding the Central Anatolian Plateau. The legendary resting place of Noah's Ark, Mount Ararat, at 16,945 feet, is found in eastern Turkey.

Climate

Within this realm hot and dry weather dominates, with some Mediterranean climate along the coasts. In the mountain regions, high peaks are snow-covered and winters are cold. The highest temperature, 136°F, was recorded at Al-Aziziyah, Libya. Rainfall throughout can run from 4 inches per year in the desert and steppe regions to more than 30 inches at higher elevations. In the Sahara, rainfall is generally less than 1 inch per year.

Flora and Fauna

Some animals and birds found in this realm include the crocodile and ibis in Egypt as well as the Bactrian camel in the central Asian deserts and the dromedary in the Saharan Desert areas. Ostrich and oryx can be found in the Arabian Peninsula. The Eurasian steppes contain some unique varieties: Saiga antelope, Przewalski's horse—the only authentic wild horse still living—and the great bustard. The Barbary ape, porcupine, fennec, acudad, jerboa, Dorcas and Dama gazelles inhabit North Africa. The warm waters of the Red Sea provide a perfect habitat for a variety of spectacular corals. The nearly extinct snow leopard and leopard, goitered gazelle, markhor goat, and Bactrian deer frequent Afghanistan. In Turkey, the Angora goat lives on the central plateau. Israel has a diverse population of birds and animals, including coneys, ibex, leopards, hyenas, and typical desert reptiles such as geckos and vipers. The sturgeon in the Caspian Sea are important commercial fish noted for their superior caviar.

The desert climate predominates in the realm, producing plant life ranging from palm trees in the Sahara oases to acacia in the wadis. Scrub brush and thorny bushes dot some areas, although parts of the desert known as *reg*, or pebble desert, are without plants. Cedars grow in Israel and Lebanon along the Mediterranean. The grasslands form the second-largest area in the realm, with several species of grass, including sheep's fescue, stipa grass, and crested wheatgrass. In the spring the rains bring dwarf iris, daisies, peonies, and hyacinths to the steppe. Of the trees that grow in the mountain areas, birch, oak, fir, hornbeam, and Caucasian elm are the most notable varieties.

Unique Features

Islam, one of the world's three major religions that began in Jerusalem (Islam, Judaism, and Christianity), is dominant throughout the realm. Conflict has been waged among these three religious groups for centuries. Nomadic people such as the Bedouins and Kurds traditionally live in tents and move about searching for food and water for their herds. Arabic is the uniform language of North Africa. Forms of ancient Persian, Turkish, and Hebrew languages are spoken in specific areas. Oil and natural gas are important natural resources, driving the economies of several countries in the realm.

 # Mapping

 ## *Bill and Pete Go Down the Nile*

Projection:	*Bill and Pete Go Down the Nile* by Tomie dePaola, 1996
Genre:	Picture Storybook
Level:	Primary (K–2)
Elements:	I. The World in Spatial Terms; II. Places and Regions; III. Physical Systems
Themes:	Location; Place; Region

The Book

Bill, a crocodile, and his ride-the-back bird friend, Pete, had lessons about their country, Egypt, from their schoolteacher, Ms. Ibis. She led a class trip down the Nile so the crocodiles and birds could view all the things they had learned about, such as the Sphinx.

The class visited a museum inside a pyramid and saw mummies, sarcophagi, and the famous bad-luck jewel known as the Sacred Eye of Ibis. Pete foiled an attempted robbery of the jewel, and the class was rewarded with a trip home on a boat.

Key Understandings

The Nile River and its fertile banks and delta provide Egyptians with a livelihood, means of transportation, and a direct link to their history.

Knowledge

- Identify the animals and vegetation in and along the Nile River in Egypt.
- Describe the historical monuments located along the Nile.
- Identify the purposes and sections of a pyramid, including the original contents.
- Describe the various types of river vessels and their uses.
- Explain the importance of the Nile River to the Egyptians.

Skills

- Ask questions about the location and extent of the Nile River.
- Ask questions about the Egyptians who live and work along the Nile.
- Inquire about the historical monuments, including the pyramids and their mummies.
- Gather information about life along the Nile.
- Categorize information on a Nile River map.
- Formulate conclusions about the Nile River Valley and its importance to the Egyptians.

Perspectives

Appreciate the central role that the Nile River, the largest river in the world, plays in the lives of those who live along it.

Activities

I = Individual   P = Pairs   G = Group

A. NILE RIVER JOURNEY MAP (P)

Materials: globe, wall map of Egypt, reproducible map of the Nile River basin, crayons, 11 x 14-inch copy paper

Using the globe, help the students locate Egypt and the Nile River. Find the Nile on the wall map of Egypt, noting its size and location. Help students determine where Cairo is. On the enlarged reproducible map, students should color the river blue, the adjacent land and delta green, and the rest of the land brown. Complete the key by filling in the boxes in the appropriate colors. Label the Nile River, Cairo, and Egypt.

Questions to Ask

1. On which continent is the Nile River located? Where is Egypt on this continent?
2. Does the Nile flow all the way through Egypt?
3. Where is Cairo located on the Nile River map?
4. What colors are used for land and water?
5. Why do you think the land near the river is green while the land farther away is light brown?

B. NILE RIVER JOURNEY SIGHTS (P)

Materials: construction paper, crayons, pencils, scissors, white glue, National Geographic World, trade books with information about Egypt and the Nile, reproducible Nile map and objects, wall map

Students should review materials for information on river vessels, animals, and vegetation found on or along the river. Have students identify on the wall map the location of pyramids and the Sphinx (see Figures 6.1 and 6.2 on pages 68 and 69) as seen on Bill and Pete's Nile journey. Color and cut out the pyramids and the Sphinx and glue them on the journey map in the appropriate places. Color the crocodiles and ibises and place them on the map. Draw and color in any vegetation and buildings along the banks. Partners should choose a vessel on which to travel on their sightseeing journey and draw it in the vessel box on the reproducible map. Acting as tour guides, take another pair on your Nile River journey, explaining the importance of the Nile to the Egyptians.

C. MUMMIES' MYSTERY (G)

Materials: construction-paper direction signs, small doll, gauze strips, pictures of mummies, adhesive tape, scissors

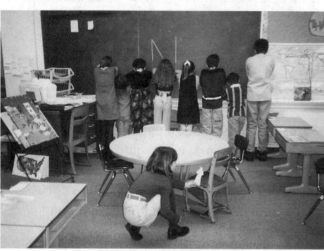

Wrapping the mummy (above). Hiding the mummy (below).

The class should be divided into groups of three to four students. Using pictures of mummies as examples, each group wraps a small doll in strips of gauze. Use adhesive tape to keep the mummy doll wrapped securely. The groups will be responsible for naming the mummies. The teacher must create signs for the cardinal directions and place them on the appropriate walls. Explain that the classroom is the interior of a pyramid where mummies have been kept hidden for many years. The teacher will determine where each group's mummy will be hidden. Now the students are ready to play the "Mummies' Mystery" game.

The Game

1. Draw a mummy's name from the sarcophagus box.
2. The group that wrapped and named the mummy leaves the classroom.
3. Hide the mummy in full view of the rest of the class.
4. The group reenters the classroom in the role of archaeologists searching for the mummy.
5. Provide five minutes to find the ancient mummy.
6. The archaeologists must ask questions of the rest of the class, using cardinal direction, location, and distance terms.
7. Keep score by recording the amount of time each group takes to find the mummy.
8. The group with the shortest time is the winner.

 # Ali, Child of the Desert

Projection:	*Ali, Child of the Desert* by Jonathan London, 1997
Genre:	Picture Storybook
Level:	Bridge (2–4)
Elements:	I. The World in Spatial Terms; II. Places and Regions; III. Physical Systems; V. Environment and Society
Themes:	Location; Place; Region; Human/Environment Interaction

The Book

Ali had finally become old enough to make the yearly trek to market through the Sahara Desert to Rissani, Morocco. He and his father were taking a camel herd to sell. The desert is brought alive to the reader through descriptive portraits of the hot sun, Ali's thirst, and a sandstorm. Ali was separated from the herd and his father during the sandstorm. He was befriended by Abdul, a Berber goatherd, as night was beginning to fall across the desert. Abdul took Ali to his oasis, where he gave him tea and told him stories about the warrior-tribesmen of Berber. Before Abdul left to take his herd to the Atlas Mountains, he gave Ali a musket to shoot hourly so that his father could find him. After a day alone in the hot desert, Ali's father finally heard the gunshot and followed the sound to him.

Key Understandings

People of the Sahara have adapted their lifestyle to fit the desert environment and meet their human needs. Food, clothing, abodes, and activities have been modified to fit the desert's harsh realities.

Knowledge

- Locate the Sahara Desert, the countries and cities that lie within its boundaries, and the Atlas Mountains.
- Describe the environment of Ali's world.
- Retell the dangers that Ali faced when he was lost in the desert.
- Compare the desert life that Ali experienced to your own personal life.

Skills

- Ask questions about the physical environment of the Sahara Desert and about desert life.
- Ask questions about how Ali adapts to this environment.
- Find information about the location, climate, and ecosystem of Ali's world.
- Organize and analyze Ali's world by categorizing it into clothing, transportation, abodes, food, and occupations.
- Categorize information about the Sahara according to climate, vegetation, and animals.
- Draw conclusions about how the desert people have adapted to the environment of the Sahara.
- Compare these adaptations to those made by people living in your own area.

Perspectives

Appreciate the ways in which the desert people have adapted to the particularly harsh environment of the Sahara Desert.

Activities

I = Individual   P = Pairs   G = Group

A. WANDERING THROUGH ALI'S DESERT (P)

Materials: physical and political wall map of North Africa, poster board, poster paints, black marking pen, pencil, sand, string, scissors, white glue, spray glue

Locate the Sahara Desert and surrounding area on the large wall map, noting the land forms, water, countries and their capitals, and Rissani. Draw, freehand with a pencil on the poster board, the outline of North Africa and its nations. Find the fringes of the Sahara and draw that as well. Paint the water along the coastal areas and the rivers blue, and label it. Land outside the desert should be painted green. Mark any mountains with variations of green and use markers to label them. Using the spray glue, coat the desert area and sprinkle sand in varying layers to represent flat areas and different dune types. Add other specimens, such as pebbles, that are likely to be found in this environment. Form the boundaries of each country with string covered with glue. Choose a color for each country and a number for each capital. Develop a key that lists the countries and capitals with the matching color and number. Add a compass rose. Label Rissani and title the map.

Questions to Ask

1. What countries are included in North Africa?
2. Which countries are wholly or partly covered by desert?
3. What land forms and cities did you find both within the desert and in the surrounding areas?
4. Where are most of the cities located? Why?
5. What is the relative and absolute location of Rissani?
6. Using the information provided in the book and your specimen map, where do you estimate that Ali and his father began their trip? Provide a rationale for your calculation.

B. Stormy Weather (G)

Materials: globe, outline map of the world, encyclopedia, atlas, colored pencils, black marker

Have the students find information about the climate regions of the world. Identify the broad areas of the world that are covered by the specific climate regions. Place the general location information on the chart next to the appropriate climate. Research the type of storms prevalent in each of the climate regions and complete the storm section of the chart. Using the outline map of the world and colored pencils, develop a climate key, choosing a different color for each one. Matching the colors, fill in the world climate map based on the information that is organized on the chart. Students should create symbols for each specific storm and create a storm key for the map. Label the climate areas with the appropriate storm symbols. Title the map and add a compass rose. Compare the stormy weather for your climate region to that of Ali's.

C. Desert Dunes Cartoons (I)

Materials: paper, wide cash-register tape, pencil, colored markers, atlas, trade books, geography books, National Geographic magazines, newspaper cartoons

Find information concerning life on the Sahara, including food, clothing, abodes, transportation, occupations, recreation, resources, and the like. Students should review newspaper cartoons to familiarize themselves with the typical cartoon style, story-line sequence, and characters. Design a cartoon strip that would include any area of a typical desert lifestyle. Transfer to the cash-register tape and display.

Neve Shalom Wahat al-Salaam: Oasis of Peace

Projection:	*Neve Shalom Wahat al-Salaam: Oasis of Peace* by Laurie Dolphin, 1993.
Genre:	Information Book
Level:	Bridge; Intermediate (2–6)
Elements:	I. The World in Spatial Terms; II. Places and Regions; IV. Human Systems
Themes:	Location; Place; Region; Movement

The Book

In Israel, a land often in conflict or war, Arabs and Jews live together in a tenuous relationship. Through photographs and text, the reader is introduced to two boys: Shlomo, a Jew, and Muhammed, an Arab. They attended a special bilingual and bicultural school where Arab and Jewish children studied together. Although they lived with their families in separate villages and practiced different religions, in this school located in the Oasis of Peace the boys learned to be friends with one another. Their homes, families, schools and school days, villages, and recreational activities are presented. A history, glossary, and language comparison are provided to help the reader better understand these very different cultures.

Key Understandings

The struggle for possession of the land of Israel has led to conflict and war among religious groups for centuries. Despite this, many people in Israel attempt to create an "oasis of peace" among the conflicting groups.

Knowledge

- Identify the relative location of Israel, the villages where Shlomo and Muhammed live, and the Neoveh Shalom/Waaohat al-Salaam where they go to school.

- Describe the environment in which Shlomo and Muhammed live.
- Explain what their lives are like in their separate villages and in this special school.
- Compare the lifestyles of the two boys.

Skills

- Ask questions about the physical environment and location of Israel and the boys' villages.
- Ask questions about their family life and school.
- Gather information about relative location, environment, and life in Israel.
- Draw comparisons between the location, environment, and life in Israel to those of the students.
- Predict the effect of the "oasis of peace" school on the future of peace in Israel.

Perspectives

Appreciate the attempts of people to coexist peaceably in a land divided by culture and religion.

Activities

I = Individual   P = Pairs   G = Group

A. MAPPING NEIGHBORS (I)

Materials: atlas, enlarged copies of Middle East map, wall map of the Middle East, card stock, 11 x 14-inch cardboard, tracing paper, scissors, markers, colored pencils

Locate the Middle East on the wall map; find Israel and adjacent countries. Using the atlas, find the map of the Middle East and enlarge so that it fits on 11 x 14-inch paper. Have students trace the outline of each country and transfer to card stock and label. Cut around the outside of each country on the card stock. Glue the enlarged copy of the map of the Middle East to the cardboard. Match each country on the card stock to the shapes on the cardboard.

Questions to Ask

1. Which countries touch Israel's borders?
2. What other Middle East countries do not touch Israel's borders?
3. Which countries are among the largest, and which are the smallest?
4. What is the size of Israel in square miles? How does that compare to other bordering countries?
5. How could the shape and size of Israel put that country in jeopardy during times of conflict?

B. FAMILIAR FAMILIES (I)

Materials: computer, Internet access, pen-pal e-mail addresses, printer

Using education sites for pen pals, have students select a pen pal in Israel. Try to ensure that the students have both Arab and Jewish pen pals in order to get a more diverse point of view. They should be able to converse about their lives at home and in their communities. Gather information about occupations, habitat, abodes, traditional foods, entertainment and sports, friends, and school life. Have students compare their family life to that of the Arab or Jewish pen pal. Students should write stories that include themselves and their pen pals, comparing their lives as the book did with Shlomo and Muhammed and including illustrations and any pictures that have been transmitted.

C. PEACE DILEMMA (G)

Materials: paper, pencils

Have groups of three to four students create an open-ended story with a problem. This problem should focus on personal territory (e.g., my room, my yard). The story should include the same number of characters as group members. The students will role-play the conflict for the rest of the class. Brainstorm and record the possible solutions with the class. In their groups the students will evaluate the consequences of each solution and formulate their own solutions to the conflict. Using what they know about resolving a dilemma over personal territory and information gathered from their pen pals, students should predict the efficacy of the "oasis of peace" school for promoting peace in Israel.

Figure 6.1–Nile River Map

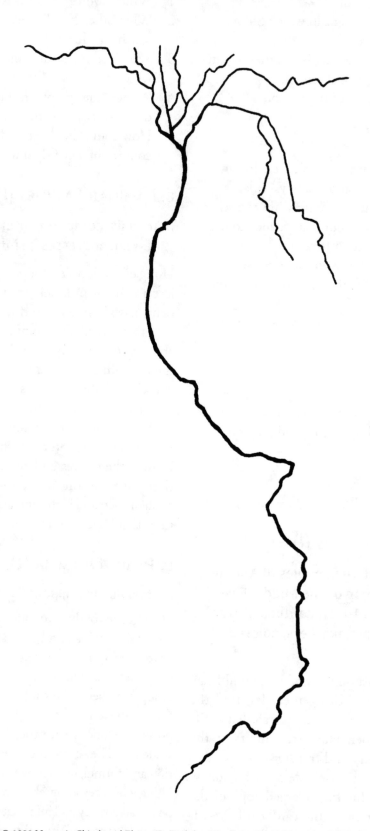

Figure 6.2—Nile River Objects

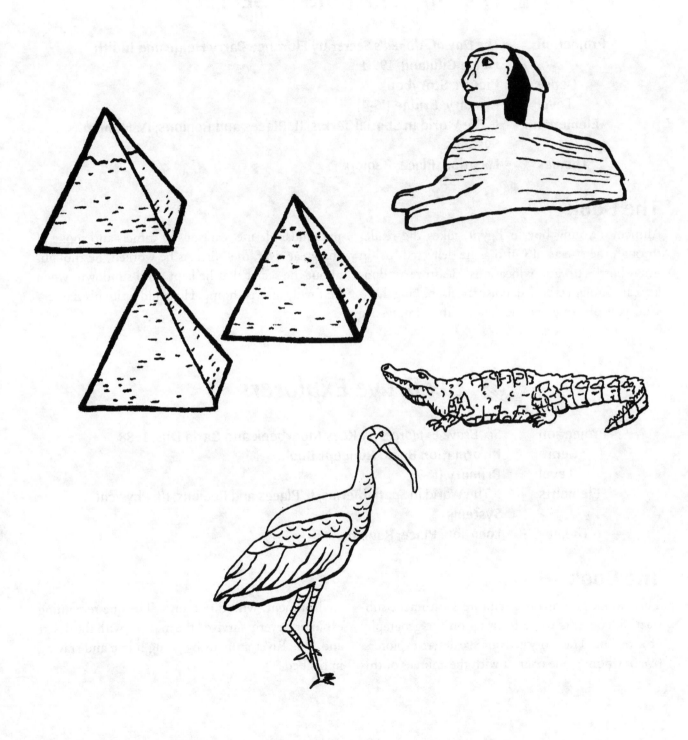

Charting with More Books

 ## *The Day of Ahmed's Secret*

Projection:	*The Day of Ahmed's Secret* by Florence Parry Heide and Judith Heide Gilliland, 1990
Genre:	Picture Storybook
Level:	Primary; Bridge (K–4)
Elements:	I. The World in Spatial Terms; II. Places and Regions; IV. Human Systems
Themes:	Location; Place; Region

The Book

Ahmed, a young boy in Egypt, takes the reader through the streets of Cairo as he delivered fuel in heavy bottles to various locations. He drove his donkey cart through crowded, noisy streets, passing thousand-year-old walls and the desert with its impressive pyramids. He met caravans of camels and spoke of the great river, the Nile. As he worked, he thought about the secret that he kept until sundown, when he finally arrived home. He could write his name!

 ## *Six Brave Explorers*

Projection:	*Six Brave Explorers* by Kees Moerbeek and Carla Dijs, 1988
Genre:	Information Book; Concept Book
Level:	Primary (K–2)
Elements:	I. The World in Spatial Terms; II. Places and Regions; III. Physical Systems
Themes:	Location; Place; Region

The Book

This unique pop-up book reinforces arithmetic subtraction concepts while focusing on the geography of a region. The story tells of six desert explorers, five of whom made contact with the animals of this environment, with dire results. The one remaining explorer cleverly survived the meeting with the desert and Nile River animals by going home and staying in his bed.

The Children of Mauritania: Days in the Desert and by the River Shore

Projection:	*The Children of Mauritania: Days in the Desert and by the River Shore* by Lauren Goldsmith, 1993
Genre:	**Information Book**
Level:	**Intermediate (4–6)**
Elements:	**I. The World in Spatial Terms; II. Places and Regions; IV. Human Systems; V. Environment and Society**
Themes:	**Location; Place; Region; Human/Environment Interaction**

The Book

Mauritania is situated in the conversion zone where the desert of North Africa meets the savannah grassland of the Western Subsaharan Desert. It is also the setting of two distinct African cultures: Arab and Black African. The reader is provided a view of these two cultures through the lives of an Arab girl, Fatimatou, and a Black African boy, Hamadi. Fatimatou and her family were Muslim desert dwellers who lived in a tent. She didn't go to school, though she read and wrote Arabic. After she cooked the meals, and took care of the goat herd, she visited with friends, eating dates, playing cards, and painting her hands and feet. Though she went to the village market, she preferred the quieter, cleaner desert. Hamadi's family lived in four houses bordering the river, which served as a gathering place for bathing and doing laundry. He went to the village school, where the language was French. He liked to play games such as soccer with his friends. Both families appeared to accommodate to their physical environment.

The Mystery of the Kaifeng Scroll

Projection:	*The Mystery of the Kaifeng Scroll* by Harriet K. Fedder, 1995
Genre:	**Fiction; Chapter Book**
Level:	**Intermediate (4–6)**
Elements:	**II. Places and Regions; IV. Human Systems; VI. The Uses of Geography**
Themes:	**Place; Region; Movement; Human/Environment Interaction**

The Book

Vivi Hartman, a schoolgirl from Buffalo, flew to Turkey to spend the summer touring the country with her mother, a professor. Arriving in Istanbul, she was dismayed to find that her mother, Dr. Davis, was not there. Vivi discovered that her mother was being held by Arab terrorists. Vivi was forced to be the pawn to get information that only her mother possessed about the ancient Kaifeng Scroll. Using shrewdness and deception, Vivi brought about the defeat of the terrorists and rescued both her mother and the ancient scroll. Mother and daughter spent the summer enjoying the sights and sounds of Turkey.

The Never-Ending Greenness

Projection:	*The Never-Ending Greenness* by Neil Waldman, 1997
Genre:	Picture Storybook
Level:	Bridge (2–4)
Elements:	I. The World in Spatial Terms; II. Places and Regions; III. Physical Systems; IV. Human Systems; V. Environment and Society
Themes:	Location; Place; Region; Movement; Human/Environment Interaction

The Book

A Jewish family living in Vilna escaped the Nazis and made a home in Israel. The little boy missed the trees that had lined the streets of his former home. He discovered a newborn tree among some rocks and nurtured it until it began to grow. Happy with his success, he searched every day in the rocks and crevices for tree seedlings, which he planted near his home. Soon there was a beautiful grove of trees. As the years passed, the little boy continued to plant the seedlings and cultivate the groves in the surrounding hills. This tradition is continued today by children from all over the world who send seedlings to Israel for planting. The never-ending greenness of Israel continues.

Realm References

dePaola, T. 1996. *Bill and Pete Go Down the Nile.* New York: The Putnam and Grosset Group.

Dolphin, L. 1993. *Neve Shalom Wahat al-Salaam: Oasis of Peace.* New York: Scholastic.

Feder, H. K. 1995. *The Mystery of the Kaifeng Scroll.* Minneapolis, MN: Lerner Publications.

Goldsmith, L. 1993. *The Children of Mauritania: Days in the Desert and by the River Shore.* Minneapolis, MN: Carolrhoda Books.

Heide, F. P., and J. H. Gilliland. 1990. *The Day of Ahmed's Secret.* New York: Lothrop, Lee and Shepard Books.

London, J. 1997. *Ali, Child of the Desert.* New York: Lothrop, Lee and Shepard Books.

Moerbeek, K., and C. Dijs. 1988. *Six Brave Explorers.* Los Angeles, CA: Price Stern Sloan.

Waldman, N. 1997. *The Never-Ending Greenness.* New York: Morrow Junior Books.

Chapter 7
Subsaharan African Realm

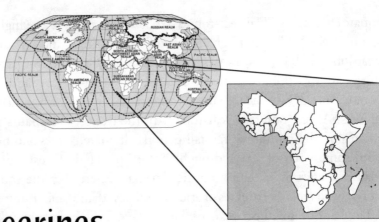

 Getting Your Bearings

Location

More than forty countries of various sizes make up this realm. The largest country on the continent of Africa is Sudan, located in both North and Subsaharan Africa, covering 967,493 square miles; the smallest, Seychelles, is a 108-square-mile island country located off the east coast of Africa in the Indian Ocean. In the northern part of the Subsaharan realm, a transition area marked by gradual changes joins North and Subsaharan Africa. Some countries that are wholly or partially included in this zone are Senegal, Gambia, Mali, Burkina Faso, Benin, Niger, Nigeria, Chad, Sudan, Eritriea, Ethiopia, Djibouti, and Somalia. The Subsaharan African Realm is divided into four regions: West, Central, East, and South. West Africa, which stretches from the Atlantic on the west and Cameroon in Central Africa, contains numerous countries, with Nigeria being the largest. The Atlantic Ocean forms the western border of Central Africa, and the Indian Ocean is the eastern border of East Africa. East Africa stretches from Ethiopia on the north through Tanzania on the south. South Africa forms the base of the continent, where the Atlantic and Indian Oceans converge at the Cape of Good Hope, and includes the countries of South Africa, Namibia, Angola, Zambia, Zimbabwe, Malawi, Botswana, and Mozambique. Madagascar, the world's fourth-largest island and the realm's largest island country, lies 250 miles off the southeast coast of Africa. Lagos, Nigeria, is by far the largest major city of this realm, with a population of 11.9 million. Political disputes have kept this realm and its countries in a state of flux.

Topography

The continent of Africa is unique in that it is one large plateau. As a result there are no north-south mountain ranges and only a few ranges in the far south, the Cape Ranges, and in Ethiopia. In the Ethiopian Highlands, volcanic activity produced the highest peaks: Kilimanjaro (Tanzania) at 19,341 feet and Mount Kenya at 17,058. The longest river in the realm is the Zaire/Congo at more than 2,700 miles, the foundation for the Congo basin. In East Africa is a chain of deep lakes formed in the bottom of the deep valleys of the Great African Rift. Lake Tanganyika, at 410 miles long and more than 4,000 feet deep, is the longest freshwater lake in the world. Lying between two rift valleys, shallow Lake Victoria, the largest lake of the realm, covers more than 26,000 square miles. On the Zambezi River, between Zambia and Zimbabwe, is one of the world's most spectacular waterfalls at over 1 mile wide and 355 feet high, Victoria Falls. Other waterfalls and gorges have been eroded by rivers and weathering into the plateau to provide variation in the landscape.

Climate

The equator passes through the center of this realm, influencing rainfall and temperature and creating a tropical climate in most parts. The tropics preclude drastic climate change, with temperatures near the equator averaging 75°F year-round. Cooler areas are found in the Ethiopian Highlands and South Africa near Johannesburg. The hottest place in the world is northeastern Ethiopia, with an average daily temperature of 93°F. In the rain forests and coastal areas of West Africa, rain falls year-round. In the rest of the realm, dry and heavy-rainfall periods alternate, with some years of severe drought occurring. The Namib Desert of Namibia and the Kalahari Desert in Botswana reflect extremes of aridity, with less than 10 inches of rainfall per year.

Flora and Fauna

An amazing variety of wildlife, many species endangered, may be found in this realm. The mountain gorilla, found in Volcanoes National Park in Rwanda, is one of the most endangered, with fewer than six hundred animals remaining in the wild. Poaching seriously threatens the gorilla and the black rhinoceros as well. The hippopotamus, an abundant water animal, is found in the lakes, ponds, rivers, and marshes of the African interior. Among large water birds, flamingos, which breed in the lakes of the rift, pelicans, and storks inhabit the East African region.

In the highest mountain forests are eagles, vultures, and buzzards. Many multicolored birds such as the sunbird inhabit the mountains, rain forests, and grasslands. Zebras, giraffes, hyenas, cheetahs, leopards, and lions roam the grasslands. Baboons and elephants prefer the mountain regions. Chimpanzees and monkeys may be found in the central rain forests. Lemurs are found mainly in Madagascar. In the equatorial countries of this realm is found a rain forest that contains a variety of trees: ebony, mahogany, okoume, oil palms, and fruit trees. In the mountain areas, camphor, juniper, African olive, and podocarp trees are notable. Two important grassland trees are the giant baobab and the acacia.

Unique Features

In this realm, over one thousand languages are spoken. Among these are three major language families, of which the Niger-Congo is the largest. Swahili is the most widely used Bantu language in this family. Malagasy, a Malayo-Polynesian family language, is spoken by the people of Madagascar. With over eight hundred ethnic groups, the Subsaharan realm is most culturally diverse.

Mapping

Come with Me to Africa: A Photographic Journey

Projection:	*Come with Me to Africa: A Photographic Journey* by Gregory Scott Kreikemeier, 1993
Genre:	Information Book
Level:	Intermediate (4–6)
Elements:	I. The World in Spatial Terms; II. Places and Regions; III. Physical Systems; IV. Human Systems; VI. The Uses of Geography
Themes:	Location; Place; Region

The Book

This photographic journey provides the reader with a snapshot of both the cultural and the physical geogra-

phy of the continent of Africa. The author prepares readers for the trip by providing a list of personal gear and expedition equipment to be placed on a specially designed truck. The six-month expedition began in the North African country of Morocco and wound its way through Central and East Africa, ending in Zimbabwe. For each of the countries visited there are pictures of the breathtaking landscape, characteristic animals, and peoples of the many cultures. The physical environment, harsh weather, animal encounters, and limited road system provided many perils that impeded travel for the expedition. Despite the hazards, the travelers had a wonderful experience because of the friendliness of the people, the magnificent vistas, and the majesty of the animals.

Key Understandings

Africa's geographic location and features, as well as its history of colonization, have contributed to the creation of a large number of countries with a broad range of diverse cultures, ethnic groups, and languages.

Knowledge

- Describe the countries through which the expedition traveled.
- Identify the flora, fauna, and natural resources of the countries traveled.
- Identify the cultural landscapes throughout the tour.
- Design a tour map depicting a trip through several countries of Africa.
- Formulate comparisons of the geographic features, animals, plant life, and peoples of several countries.

Skills

- Generate questions about the geographic location and features as well as colonial history of the countries visited during photo safari.
- To create a personal safari, ask similar questions about other locations.
- Gather information through pictures and printed materials from library and Internet sources.

- Organize pictures and materials into a tour map and journey.
- Make comparisons among the countries on the journey of the physical and cultural landscapes.
- Draw conclusions about the diversity of the continent of Africa.

Perspectives

Appreciate the variety of the cultural and physical landscapes of Africa.

Activities

I = Individual   P = Pairs   G = Group

A. Our Subsaharan Safari (P)

Materials: atlas, wall map of Africa, encyclopedia, *National Geographic*, geography books, outline map of Africa, colored pencils, markers

Have students find Africa in the atlas and on a wall map. Choose at least three countries through which to travel on the safari. From the outline map, make an enlargement of the selected countries. Collect some data about the physical and political geography of the selected countries. Determine the sites that are important to visit within these countries. Plot a route that is accessible for the tourist wishing to travel to these sites. Label capitals and other major cities, geographic features, and notable sites. Add a legend that identifies capitals, physical features, and political boundaries. Place a scale of miles and kilometers on the map as well as a compass rose that includes intermediate directions. Title it "Our Subsaharan Safari."

Questions to Ask

1. What is the size of the continent of Africa? How many countries can you find?
2. Between what lines of latitude and longitude are your safari countries located? What is the relative location?
3. What are the capitals and major cities of these countries?

4. Where are the geographic features and notable sites located within each country?

5. How many miles and kilometers will the tourist cover in order to complete your safari? How does your mileage compare to the mileage of the expedition in the book?

B. INTERNET SAFARI BROCHURE (P)

Materials: computer, Internet access, color Inkjet or laser printer, legal-size or larger paper

Using the World Wide Web, the students should gather information and pictures about the countries identified in "Our Subsaharan Safari." Special attention should be given to the peoples and cultures found in each of the countries. For each country, gather information on demographics (vital statistics), geographic sites, flora and fauna, and cultural features. Design a four-fold brochure, including a title page, a guide to safari preparation (transportation, gear), and a description of each country, with pictures and information. Following the steps for cutting and pasting information and pictures from the Internet, complete a safari brochure that reflects the cultural and physical landscape of "Our Subsaharan Safari."

C. RESOURCE PASSPORT (P)

Materials: copy of a U.S. passport, school picture, paper, card stock, stapler, blocks of wood, glue, rubber, stamp ink pad, atlas, encyclopedia

Using a copy of a passport as a guide, have students create their own passports, resembling the model as much as possible. Then research information about the resources of the countries through which the safari passes and determine the most important ones. Create symbols that represent the most important resource for each country, and cut the rubber material in those shapes. Glue each shape to one end of the wooden block. Stamp the resources for each country in the passport. Present information to the class about the country, its resources, and their relationship to colonization.

 # The Village of Round and Square Houses

Projection:	*The Village of Round and Square Houses* by Ann Grifalconi, 1986
Genre:	Picture Storybook
Level:	Primary (K–2)
Elements:	I. The World in Spatial Terms; II. Places and Regions; IV. Human Systems; V. Environment and Society
Themes:	Location; Place; Human/Environment Interaction

The Book

At the foot of Naka Mountain in West Africa lies Tos, the isolated village of round and square houses. How this unique village came about is told by a woman who grew up there. She relates the tale of how old Naka erupted one night, spewing lava. In the morning, the villagers were covered with gray ash and the burned-out village had only two remaining houses, a square one and a round one. Believing this to be a sign from old Naka, the chief sent all the men to the square house, the women to the round house, and the children to clear little stones from the fields. So it remained, and the men and the women liked to spend their time talking, singing, and working in their respective round and square houses. The villagers lived peaceably this way for all had a time to be apart and a time to be together.

Key Understandings

People create cultural traditions that help them adapt to physical conditions in their environment. The tradition of the round and square houses of the village grew out of the physical impact the volcano had on the community.

Knowledge

- Locate the continent of Africa and the country of Cameroon.
- Describe the village of Tos and the surrounding environment.
- Explain the results of the eruption of Naka on the villagers' lives.
- Compare the village of Tos to the students' local community.

Skills

- Ask questions about the location of Africa and Cameroon.
- Ask questions about Tos and the surrounding environment.
- Gather information concerning abodes, landscape, and the natural hazard of Naka.
- Organize information into a map and diorama.
- Categorize abodes according to shapes.
- Determine how the village of round and square houses came to be.

Perspectives

Appreciate the geographic origin of the tradition of the people of Tos living in round and square houses.

Activities

I = Individual   P = Pairs   G = Group

A. UNCOVERING CAMEROON (I)

Materials: inflatable globe, wall map of Africa, outline map of Africa, crayons

On the inflatable globe, have students locate the continent of Africa by tracing its outline and identifying the Atlantic Ocean. Find the country of Cameroon on the political wall map of Africa, noting its location relative to the Atlantic Ocean. Determine on which side of the continent of Africa Cameroon is located, using cardinal directions. On the outline map of Africa color Cameroon and outline the border. Color the rest of the continent a different color. Create the cardinal directions by making a cross and labeling north, south, east, and west.

Questions to Ask

1. Is Africa on the same side of the globe as North America?
2. What does the shape of Africa look like? Is Africa shaped like North America? How is it the same? How is it different?
3. On which side of Africa is Cameroon located?
4. Is there water near Cameroon? What is this body of water?

B. VIEWING THE VILLAGE (P)

Materials: shoebox, construction paper of various colors, crayons, scissors, white glue, small round cans, wooden blocks, roof patterns (square and round)

Using the pictures in the book as a guide, have students determine the objects that will best represent Tos in a diorama. Put the background landscape on the back and the bottom of the shoebox with crayons

Making village houses.

and construction paper. Using the roof patterns, make square and round roofs for the block and small can. Cover the can and block with construction paper and add the appropriate roof. Place the round and square houses in the diorama. Design and include in the diorama any other details, such as trees and animals. Display the diorama in the classroom.

C. THE SHAPES IN MY COMMUNITY

Materials: drawing paper, crayons

Take a walk around the local community. Have the students identify the shapes of the outsides and shapes within shapes of buildings. When students return to the classroom, they should use the shapes to draw and color pictures of buildings in the community. Have them compare the shapes in their drawings to the shapes in Tos. Describe the buildings in both communities. Discuss with students the reasons for round and square houses in Tos. Have them speculate about how nature has played a role in determining the shapes of the buildings in their own community.

 # Count Your Way Through Africa

Projection:	*Count Your Way Through Africa* by Jim Haskins, 1988
Genre:	Information Book; Concept Book
Level:	Bridge (2–4)
Elements:	I. The World in Spatial Terms; II. Places and Regions; III. Physical Systems; IV. Human Systems
Themes:	Location; Place; Region

The Book

Using the Swahili language for numbers one through ten, this book presents a unique blend of information and illustrations about Africa. A syllabary is added so that readers can correctly pronounce the numbers. The concise narrative accompanying the numbers covers a wide range of physical and cultural geographic topics. The reader is introduced to Africa's location, history, landscape, animals, dance, and art.

Key Understandings

Africa is the home of a variety of animal species and cultural traditions.

Knowledge

- Locate Africa; find Subsaharan Africa, noting the countries and their national parks, game preserves, and animal sanctuaries.
- Identify the indigenous animals and traditional instruments.

- Describe the customs, art, dance, and music of the Subsaharan peoples.

Skills

- Ask questions about the types of animals and the location of their habitats.
- Ask questions about the customs, art, dance, and music of Africa.
- Formulate hypotheses about the fauna and cultures of Africa.
- Gather information and pictures and organize them into a map and collage.
- Make conclusions about the ways in which the fauna and cultures contribute to the flavor of Africa.

Perspectives

Recognize the unique contributions of the people of Africa to the world in their efforts to save their environment and preserve their traditions.

Activities

I = Individual   P = Pairs   G = Group

A. LOCATING AFRICA'S ANIMALS (P)

Materials: atlas, encyclopedia, globe, enlarged outline maps of Subsaharan Africa, pencils, colored pencils, animal pictures, glue sticks, scissors

Using the globe, find the continent of Africa and the Subsaharan countries. On the outline map, using the atlas as a guide, label the countries. Find at least one national park, preserve, or sanctuary and label its location on the map. In the encyclopedia and other books on Africa, research animals and their ranges. Gather pictures of animals that are found in these countries and glue them onto the map in the appropriate areas. Color the animals, especially in those pictures that have been copied. Label the map and add a compass rose.

Questions to Ask

1. Where is Africa located? What countries are considered Subsaharan?
2. What is the name of the park or sanctuary that you identified? In which nation is it located? Is it north or south of the equator?
3. What animals could a visitor find in your park? Are those animals found in other countries? Which ones?
4. How are these animals similar to or different from animals that are typically found around where you live?

B. CULTURAL COLLAGE (G)

Materials: magazines, card stock, poster board or tag board, white glue or paste, scissors, crayons, watercolors

Have available a variety of popular magazines (e.g., *National Geographic*) that focus on Subsaharan Africa's art, history, buildings, customs, occupations, tools, dress, foods, musical instruments, and dance. Create cards, each showing a number from one through ten in Swahili. Search through the magazines for pictures. Determine what pictures will relate to each number, keeping in mind that some categories are more difficult to find. Cut out and classify pictures according to the cultural characteristics listed above. In addition, be sure to have the appropriate number of pictures to match the selected Swahili number. Design a collage of pictures according to category on the poster board. Glue the number cards adjacent to each set of pictures. Use crayons or paint to decorate and title the poster. Report the cultural mosaic depicted in the collage to the class and make comparisons among posters.

C. MAKING AFRICAN MUSIC (G)

Materials: empty ice-cream barrels and/or round oatmeal containers, stretchable material such as latex, scissors, one-hole punch, twine, poster paint, encyclopedia, books on African musical instruments (e.g., *Multicultural Perspectives in Music Education* by W. M. Anderson and P. S. Campbell), reproducible directions for drum making

Africans of various locations have developed a variety of instruments to make music. An example is the kora in Senegal that is composed of a hollowed-out gourd, sticks, and string. The banjo has its origin in Africa as well. Using the book materials, research the different instruments used in Subsaharan Africa and select one to construct. For those interested in making drums, use the reproducible directions and follow the instructions (see Figure 7.1 on page 80). Once the instruments are completed, make African rhythms.

Figure 7.1—Making African Rhythms
Examples of Rhythmic Instruments

1. Ivory side-blown horn (Congo)

2. Raft zither (Nigeria)

3. Kalengo (Nigeria)

4. Rattle on a stick (South Africa)

5. African conical drums

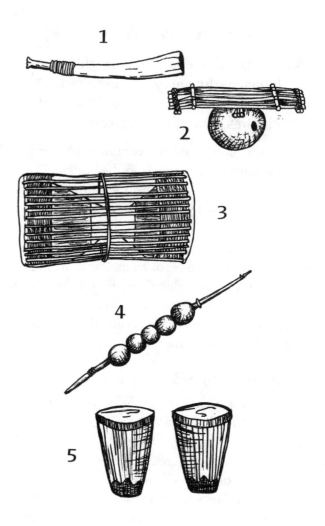

Making a Drum

1. Remove the top and carefully cut out the inside of the bottom of the cylinder.
2. Using the end of the cylinder as a pattern, mark a circle on the latex two inches larger than the carton.
3. Cut out two latex circles.
4. With a one-hole punch, make equidistant holes around the top and bottom edges of both circles.
5. Decorate the outside of the carton with poster paints.
6. Place the latex circles on the tops and bottoms of the carton.
7. Run the twine through the holes in the latex circles, going top to bottom until all holes have been used.
8. Tie ends of twine together tightly to keep the top and bottom taut.

Charting with More Books

 ## *Jambo Means Hello: Swahili Alphabet Book*

Projection:	*Jambo Means Hello: Swahili Alphabet Book* by Muriel Feelings, 1985
Genre:	Information; Alphabet Book
Level:	Bridge (2–4)
Elements:	I. The World in Spatial Terms; II. Places and Regions; IV. Human Systems
Themes:	Location; Place; Region

The Book

In Subsaharan Africa, Swahili, including its dialects, is the primary language spoken in twelve Central African countries. The book presents the twenty-four-letter alphabet of this language (*q* and *x* omitted). The reader is introduced to a word beginning with an alphabet letter, a definition, and a visual example in soft variations of gray, black, and white.

The words chosen for each letter provide a view of human and physical life in this region, including animals, plants, traditions, occupations, and amusements. The author's purpose is to foster understanding of this unique environment through language using the alphabet format.

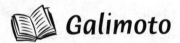 ## *Galimoto*

Projection:	*Galimoto* by Karen Lynn Williams, 1990
Genre:	Picture Storybook
Level:	Primary; Bridge (K–4)
Elements:	I. The World in Spatial Terms; II. Places and Regions; IV. Human Systems
Themes:	Location; Place; Region

The Book

A *galimoto (car* in Malawi) is a special toy fashioned from discarded wires, sticks, cornstalks, and other materials. Kondi, a seven-year-old child, decided he would make a *galimoto.* He scavenged for scraps and was accused of stealing. Finally he was allowed to keep his material, and he created a pickup truck. One night he took his *galimoto* for a run over a dusty path, and his friends all agreed that it was splendid.

Ogbo: Sharing Life in an African Village

Projection:	*Ogbo: Sharing Life in an African Village* by Ifeoma Onyefulu, 1996
Genre:	**Information Book**
Level:	**Primary; Bridge (K–4)**
Elements:	**I. The World in Spatial Terms; II. Places and Regions; IV. Human Systems**
Themes:	**Location; Place; Region**

The Book

In a village in eastern Nigeria, at the age of ten each person is assigned a responsibility according to an ogbo, which is an age group within which each child is born. The author describes life in her village through the use of terms in her native language and chores from each ogbo. Foods, clothing, celebrations, and other traditions are depicted.

 # Shadow

Projection:	*Shadow* by Marcia Brown, 1982
Genre:	**Poetry**
Level:	**Intermediate (4–6)**
Elements:	**II. Places and Regions; III. Physical Systems**
Themes:	**Place; Region; Human/Environment Interaction**

The Book

As translated and illustrated by the author, this poem introduces the reader to the frightening images of shadow, the symbol of the ghosts of the past. This spirit was ever present and everywhere. It slithered in forest and field, flitting among the animals or dancing around the campfire. Shadow had no voice nor shape but could be seen in the sparks of the fire or through the voice of the storyteller.

 # African Kingdoms of the Past

Projection:	*African Kingdoms of the Past* by Kenny Mann, 1996
Genre:	**Information Book**
Level:	**Intermediate (4–6)**
Elements:	**I. The World in Spatial Terms; II. Places and Regions; III. Physical Systems; IV. Human Systems; V. Environment and Society**
Themes:	**Location; Place; Region; Movement; Human/Environment Interaction**

The Book

In Southern Africa, during the late Iron Age, there developed three notable tribal kingdoms—Monomotapa, Zulu, and Basuto. The book chronicles the history of the rise and fall of each kingdom. Details are provided concerning powerful kingdom leaders such as Gatsi Rusere of Monomotapa, Shaka of Zulu, and Basuto's Moshueshue. The fall of these three domains is tied to their subjugation by Portuguese, British, Dutch, and German colonists who came to trade, convert, exploit resources, and live. A timeline aids the reader through the complexity of events.

 ## *My Painted House, My Friendly Chicken, and Me*

Projection:	*My Painted House, My Friendly Chicken, and Me* by Maya Angelou, 1994
Genre:	Information Book
Level:	Primary (K–2)
Elements:	I. The World in Spatial Terms; II. Places and Regions; IV. Human Systems
Themes:	Location; Place; Region

The Book

Maya Angelou presents the story of a young South African girl named Thandi. The photographs colorfully portray Thandi in the village of Ndebele, where she told secrets to her pet chicken, played with friends, and learned to paint the unique designs on the houses. Although she had to wear a uniform to school, she was happiest when wearing her traditional beaded apron and loin flap. Her life is a happy one, even if it is sometimes upset by the antics of her mischievous brother.

Realm References

Angelou, M. 1994. *My Painted House, My Friendly Chicken, and Me*. New York: Clarkson Potter.

Brown, M. 1982. *Shadow*. New York: Aladdin Books.

Feelings, M. 1985. *Jambo Means Hello: Swahili Alphabet Book*. New York: Dial Books for Children.

Grifalconi, A. 1986. *The Village of Round and Square Houses*. Boston, MA: Little, Brown.

Haskins, J. 1989. *Count Your Way Through Africa: A Photographic Journey*. Minneapolis, MN: Carolrhoda Books.

Kreikemeier, G. S. 1993. *Come with Me to Africa: A Photographic Journey*. New York: Western Publishing.

Mann, K. 1996. *African Kingdoms of the Past*. Parsippany, NJ: Dillon Press.

Onyefulu, I. 1996. *Ogbo: Sharing Life in an African Village*. San Diego, CA: Gulliver Books.

Williams, K. L. 1990. *Galimoto*. New York: Lothrop, Lee and Shepard Books.

Chapter 8

South Asian Realm

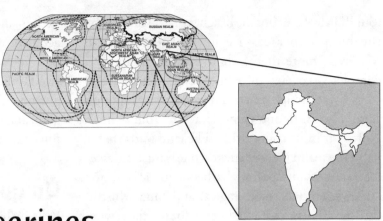

 ## Getting Your Bearings

Location

The Indian Ocean, the Arabian Sea, and the Bay of Bengal to the south and the Himalayas to the north physically rim this realm. Political entities forming the western and eastern boundaries are Iran, Afghanistan, China, and Myanmar. The most populous country, India, is the largest land mass of this realm. Other countries include Pakistan, the disputed territory of Kashmir, Nepal, Bhutan, Bangladesh, the island country of Sri Lanka, and the small, multi-island republic of Maldives. Bombay in India is the largest city of the realm with over 16.6 million people, followed, in descending order, by Calcutta, India; Karachi, Pakistan; New Delhi, India; and Dhaka, Bangladesh.

Topography

The highest mountain in the world, Mount Everest, at 29,028 feet, is located in the world's highest mountain system, the Himalayas, in the mountainous northern area of this realm. These spectacular mountains stretch across Northern India, Nepal, and Bhutan. The Karakoram Range in Jammu and Kashmir includes K–2 at 28,250 feet. Rivers in this realm form a lowland area that stretches from the Indus River in Pakistan through the Ganges Valley in India, continuing to the double delta of the Ganges and Brahmaputra in Bangladesh. South of the river lowlands are three plateaus: the Central Indian, the Chota Nagpur, and the large Deccan Plateau. Meeting the shore from the Deccan Plateau are two hill areas known as the Western and Eastern Ghats. Mountains as high as 8,000 feet are characteristic of the island nation of Sri Lanka.

Climate

The monsoon cycle dominates the climate of this realm. The warm, tropical Indian Ocean provides moisture to the seasonal winds. When the wet monsoon arrives, rain may continue for more than sixty days, bringing much-needed moisture to the hot, dry land. In northeastern India and Bangladesh, over 400 inches of rain per year may fall. In the Thar Desert (or Great Indian Desert) in Pakistan and India, rainfall is less than 10 inches per year. In the northern plain areas, some frost can occur during the cool season, October through February, but during the hot season temperatures often rise to well over 100°F. Alpine climate is typical of the high mountains of Nepal, Bhutan, India, and Pakistan.

Flora and Fauna

On the lower slopes of the Himalayas are beautiful deciduous forests of oaks; higher up, coniferous forests of cypress and cedar mix with giant rhododendrons and eventually give way to rhododendron forests. In India's forests are ebony, teak, sandalwood, and bamboo, valuable woods used for export. Along the Ganges River, mango, palm, and fig trees grow, and mangrove swamps are characteristic of the delta. On the Deccan triangle of southern India, thorny acacia trees and other bushes and small trees may be found. Palm trees dot the beaches of Sri Lanka, while the mountain areas are heavily forested. The Maldives, more than a thousand tiny islands, are completely covered by palm trees in most places.

This realm has a rich and varied animal population. The Antigone crane is a bird found in the Northern India countryside. The land birds that inhabit the realm include cuckoo pheasants, iridescent lofofor pheasants, parrots, barbets, aquatic jays, stone curlews, crested snake eagles, and blue whistling thrushes. This area is well known for the tiger, whose existence is threatened by poachers. Other predatory mammals include the dhole, a wild dog; two kinds of leopards—the spotted and the black panther; the Asian lion of the Gir forest of India; and the golden jackal. The Asian elephant, distinguished from its African cousin by smaller ears and tusks, lives in the forests of the realm. The one-horned rhinoceros resides in India and Nepal. Yaks, beasts of burden, are the lifeline for the people of Bhutan, providing food,

shelter, and fuel. A variety of antelopes are also characteristic of India; the nilgau antelope, the largest of these, almost reaches the height of a horse. There are two families of monkeys common to India: the langur, an animal sacred to followers of the Hindu religion, and the *macaca*, which includes the well-known pink-faced rhesus monkey.

Unique Features

Religion has been a major defining factor for the realm. Pakistan is an Islamic republic, while India is mostly Hindu, with a few Christians and Muslims, and the majority of the people of Bhutan and Sri Lanka are Buddhists. Population is another key feature, especially in India, Pakistan, and Bangladesh. Poverty and disease have been the unfortunate result of overpopulation in many areas. The population continues to rise every year because of high birth rates and improved health care, which keeps the death rate low.

 # Mapping

 ## *In the Heart of the Village*

Projection: ***In the Heart of the Village*** **by Barbara Bash, 1996**
Genre: **Picture Storybook**
Level: **Bridge (2–4)**
Elements: **I. The World in Spatial Terms; II. Places and Regions; V. Environment and Society; VI. The Uses of Geography**
Themes: **Place; Region; Human/Environment Interaction**

The Book

A retelling of the Indian folktale about the creation of the banyan tree introduces the story. The activities that were carried out under the banyan in the village center are presented. The people worshipped, sold their wares, rested in the shade, made agreements, and staged performances, and the children

played in the branches of the enormous banyan tree. Many animals utilized the tree as well. Egrets nested in the branches, small birds sang and ate the red figs, owls slept in the shade, and monkeys played in the branches. The banyan became the center of life for the village.

Key Understandings

There is an interdependence of flora, fauna, and human life throughout the world. In India, the banyan tree plays a central role in the daily lives of the people and animals.

Knowledge

- Describe the banyan tree, its structure and growth.
- Explain the tree's role in the lives of people in Indian villages.
- Describe the types of animals that inhabit the banyan, and relate their activities.
- Draw conclusions about the interdependence of the banyan, people, and animals.

Skills

- Ask questions about the growth and development of banyan trees.
- Ask questions about the animals that inhabit the banyan tree.
- Ask questions about human activities under the banyan tree.
- Gather information about the tree, the people, and the animals.
- Separate the information into tree, people, and animal catagories.
- Draw conclusions about the interdependence of people and animals and the banyan tree.

Perspectives

Value the interaction and interdependence of people with the environment.

Activities

I = Individual   P = Pairs   G = Group

A. BANYAN WORLD MAP (I)

Materials: globe, wall map of the world, atlas, encyclopedia, outline map of the world, construction paper, scissors, pencils, colored pencils, white glue

Locate India on the globe and wall map. Then locate the other areas in which banyan trees grow, as noted in the book. Determine similarities among the banyan tree areas in relationship to major lines of latitude. Label the Tropic of Cancer, Tropic of Capricorn, and the equator on the outline map. Label the countries where banyan trees are found. Using the colored pencils, color only those countries with banyans. Draw small pictures of banyan trees and color and cut them out. Glue the banyan trees in the areas where they are found in each of the countries.

Questions to Ask

1. What other countries border India? What ocean borders India?
2. Where else in the world does the banyan tree grow?
3. When you found the banyan trees, what did you notice about their locations throughout the world? Which lines of latitude are they closest to?
4. Why do you think banyan trees grow only in those areas?

B. BANYAN BEASTS AND BIRDS (I)

Materials: watercolors, watercolor paper, pencils, scissors, encyclopedia, National Geographic

Students must gather information about the types of animals that live in, under, and around the banyan tree in India. Each student should select one animal to draw on the watercolor paper. The teacher should ensure that a variety of animals are represented. Paint each animal in the appropriate colors. Cut out the animals and save for the "Tree Theater." Share information about the animals with classmates.

C. THE TREE THEATER (G)

Materials: colored butcher paper, leaf patterns, twigs and branches, scissors, tape, white glue, stapler, animals from "Banyan Beasts and Birds"

Using *In the Heart of the Village* as a guide, construct a banyan tree on one wall and the adjacent ceiling of the classroom. Students may fashion leaves from various-sized leaf patterns and attach them to the ceiling and wall. If branches are used, the leaves can be taped or glued to them, then attached to the ceiling in some way. Construction representing the banyan roots should be placed on either side of the proposed stage area and attached to the ceiling and the floor.

Complete the tree theater, placing the trunk and large branches on the wall in the background; add the animals to the stage set. Each group will choose a scene from the book to dramatize under the banyan. Write the script, practice, and present the scene to the class. Prepare for a presentation to other classes with a list of questions for discussion after all of the scenes are dramatized. Draw conclusions about the interdependence of people and animals with the banyan tree.

The Story of Little Babaji

Projection:	*The Story of Little Babaji* by Helen Bannerman, illustrated and retold by Fred Marcellino, 1996
Genre:	Picture Storybook
Level:	Primary (K–2)
Elements:	II. Places and Regions; III. Physical Systems
Themes:	Place; Region

The Book

The Story of Little Babaji is a retelling of Bannerman's 1899 book, *Little Black Sambo*, using authentic Indian names. Little Babaji, a young boy in India, got some brand-new clothes from his parents. Wearing his new clothes, he went walking in the jungle, where he met a series of tigers who threatened him and tricked him out of his beautiful new outfit. But Little Babaji was not so easily duped. When the tigers began to fight over which one looked best, he hid behind his umbrella and watched. The tigers were so angry that they linked tails around a palm tree and spun around so fast that they turned to *ghi*, or butter. Mamaji used the *ghi* to fry pancakes. Papaji, Mamaji, and Babaji sat down for a supper of pancakes that resembled the yellow and brown colors of the tigers.

Key Understandings

India is distinguished by the unique clothing worn by the people who inhabit the land.

Knowledge

- Describe the different types of clothing worn by Babaji, Mamaji, and Papaji.
- Identify the animals and plants peculiar to the Indian jungle habitat.
- Discuss how the others' clothing and environment are alike and different from Babaji's.

Skills

- Ask questions about Babaji's new clothes and the clothes worn by his family.
- Ask questions about the plants and animals found in Babaji's jungle and in other Indian jungles.
- Gather pictures of Babaji's environment.
- Categorize pictures according to animals, plants, and clothing.
- Determine how the animals, plants, and clothing in Babaji's environment are alike and different from those in the students' environment.

Perspectives

Appreciate the differences among people and animals in various geographic areas.

Activities

I = Individual   P = Pairs   G = Group

A. JUNIOR JUNGLE MAP (I)

Materials: primary globe, yarn, tape, drawing paper, crayons, description of Babaji's walk through the jungle from *The Story of Little Babaji*

Locate India on the globe, noting the distance from the students' location. Using the yarn with one end taped to the globe on the home location, stretch around the globe until India is reached. After listening to the story, have students make a mental map of Babaji's walk in the jungle, noting any buildings, trees, plants, and animals. After making the mental map, students should verbalize the points of interest as well as the events that occurred. Each student should choose a frame from his or her mental map to draw and share. Have students make a mental map of a walk they have taken in their own neighborhood and select a frame to draw and share.

Questions to Ask

1. Where is India in relation to where you live?
2. Is India near or far from you?
3. What plants and animals did you see in your mental jungle map?
4. What plants and animals did you see in your mental neighborhood map?

5. What things are alike and different when comparing the jungle and your neighborhood?

B. ANIMAL PUPPETS OF THE JUNGLE (I)

Materials: paper lunch bags, yarn, material scraps, buttons, construction paper, white glue, crayons, stapler, magazines (e.g., *National Geographic World*)

Have the students search in children's magazines for pictures of jungle animals peculiar to India and select one to cut out or to draw. Fold the bottom of the bag. Draw or glue the face of the animal on the bottom and the body on the rest of the bag. Place the hand inside to the bottom of the paper bag. Fold the fingers so that they reach the edge of the bottom of the bag and grasp the fold so that it touches the side of the bag. Move up and down to work the mouth of the animal. The student will have the animal introduce itself to classmates.

C. ALL DRESSED UP (P)

Materials: clothing, reproducible, 11 x 14-inch copy paper, crayons, pencils, magazines, mail-order catalogs, glue

Enlarge the reproducible (see Figure 8.1 on page 92) so that each pair has a large copy with which to work. Provide mail-order catalogs and magazines for students to select and cut out clothing from India and the United States appropriate to the categories on the reproducible. Glue the pictures in a line, left to right, next to the correct categories. Have partners present their charts and tell how the clothing is alike and different. Display in the classroom for all to see.

Shabanu: Daughter of the Wind

Projection: *Shabanu: Daughter of the Wind* by Suzanne Fisher Staples, 1989
Genre: Fiction; Chapter Book
Level: Intermediate (4–6)
Elements: I. The World in Spatial Terms; II. Places and Regions; III. Physical Systems; IV. Human Systems; V. Environment and Society
Themes: Location; Place; Region; Movement; Human/Environment Interaction

The Book

The reader is given a view of a spirited eleven-year-old girl, Shabanu, and her family, who make their livelihood herding camels in the Cholistan Desert in Pakistan. The story relates how this nomadic family survived a fierce desert storm and the relentless search for *toba*, fresh water, in this harsh but beautiful environment. Shabanu tended the herd and accompanied her father on the exciting, perilous journey to Bulachistan to bargain for the highest price for their camels. Information about the foods, clothes, religious rites, and customs of the nomadic Hindus is intertwined throughout the story. Shabanu's father arranged marriages for his daughters according to tradition in this region. She discovered that she was to marry the rich, much older Rahim-*sahib* who already had three wives. Appalled, Shabanu attempted to run away but returned home because she accepted the reality of life for a female in this culture.

Key Understandings

The environment of the Thar Desert causes its inhabitants to become nomadic, moving from place to place in order to fulfill their needs. Population density follows geographic features and climatic conditions. The South Asian realm is plagued by the problems associated with overpopulation.

Knowledge

- Identify the countries of the South Asian realm and the specific area of Shabanu's world.
- Explain the concept of population density and the issues associated with it.

- Display the populations and population densities of the countries of the realm.
- Describe the traditions of Shabanu's culture and make comparisons with one's own culture.

Skills

- Ask questions about overpopulation and its associated problems.
- Ask questions about the traditions of Islamic culture.
- Gather information from a variety of secondary and primary sources.
- Organize and analyze information into a population density map, documentary video, and presentation of customs.
- Propose possible solutions to the issues raised.

Perspectives

Empathize with Shabanu and other nomadic peoples about the harsh realities of desert life and customs. Appreciate the ways in which the South Asian people have survived in adapting to overpopulation.

Activities

I = Individual   P = Pairs   G = Group

A. REALM POPULATION MAP (I)

Materials: wall map of South Asia, geography books, encyclopedia, atlas, outline map of the realm, graph paper, colored pencils, thin marker

Locate the South Asian realm on the wall map, naming the countries that are included. Students should label the country names on the outline map. Using the atlas, have students find information about the population density and total population of each country in the realm. Create a key on the outline map that reflects the population key on the density map in the atlas. Students may choose their own key colors, but it should be noted that, generally, colors used are monochromatic. Recreate population density on the outline map, matching the key colors. Return to the atlas and find the major physical features of the realm (e.g., deserts, mountain ranges, rivers, plateaus) and label them on the map. Look up the population of each country of the realm and record. Using the graph paper, label each country of the realm on the y axis, label population numbers in intervals on the x axis (use a size that will fit as an inset on the outline map.) Matching each country to its total population, color graph bars of appropriate lengths. Cut out and glue the population bar graph in an open area on the outline map.

Questions to Ask

1. What countries make up the South Asian realm?
2. Which country has the largest population? Which has the least?
3. How would you define population density? What do you notice about the patterns of population density?
4. How are the physical features related to the density of the population?
5. Why is the population relatively sparse in Shabanu's world?

B. THE TRADITIONS OF SHABANU'S WORLD (G)

Materials: encyclopedia, supplementary multicultural trade books, Pakistan websites, cookbooks with traditional Pakistani foods, information books on Pakistan, *National Geographic*

In groups of four to five students, research Pakistani traditions like those practiced in Shabanu's world. Each group should choose one tradition to present to the class. Be sure to have a different custom for each group. Making a traditional dish for eating is an option. After

Searching for customs of traditional dress on the Internet.

presenting their custom, the group members should lead a discussion that draws comparisons between Shabanu's world and the students' world.

C. REALM REALITIES: A TELEVISION DOCUMENTARY (G)

Materials: camcorder, videotape, VCR/TV, scripts, cue cards

Have each group choose an issue that relates to population and culture of the entire realm. Gather information about the chosen issue by consulting library and Internet sources and interviewing knowledgeable people within the community. Group members should contribute information to a group script based on their findings. Each group member will take on a different role based on the needs of the production (e.g., camera operator, director, reporter, narrator). The documentary should introduce the issue, present different points of view, and draw conclusions. Rehearsal and editing will be necessary to refine the final product. Show the documentaries in class and discuss possible resolutions for each issue.

Figure 8.1–All Dressed Up

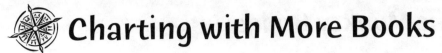 # Charting with More Books

 ## Buddha

Projection: *Buddha* by Demi, 1996
Genre: Biography
Level: Bridge; Intermediate (2–6)
Elements: II. Places and Regions; IV. Human Systems
Themes: Location; Place; Region

The Book

It is told that hundreds of years ago in India, Prince Siddhartha was born into a life of opulence. As a young man, Siddhartha was curious about people outside the palace. Determined to see for himself, he encountered suffering, sorrow, and death. To seek the truth of life over death and to find inner peace, he became a monk. After searching for years, he rested under a bodhi tree, where he underwent enlightenment and saw the whole mystery of life. At age thirty-five he became a buddha and spent his life teaching the eight-fold path to enlightenment.

 ## Kanu of Kathmandu: A Journey in Nepal

Projection: *Kanu of Kathmandu: A Journey in Nepal* by Barbara A. Margolies, 1992
Genre: Information Book
Level: Bridge (2–4)
Elements: I. The World in Spatial Terms; II. Places and Regions; IV. Human Systems; V. Environment and Society
Themes: Place; Region; Human/Environment Interaction

The Book

The story of Nepal is told by Kanu, who lived in Kathmandu, the capital. Kanu related information about his country through a tour of the countryside and cities. Among the tour sights were farms on which people grew fruits, vegetables, and grains; schools that were all private; and games being played by children whose families could not afford to send them to school. The homes and trucks were adorned with delightful designs. There were interesting and ancient temples, Hindu and Buddhist, in the cities. Upon returning to Kathmandu, Kanu described the busy streets and diverse peoples who frequented them. While at home, he dreamed about someday climbing one of the very high mountains in the Himalayas.

 # *The Monkey Bridge*

Projection:	*The Monkey Bridge* **retold by Rafe Martin, 1997**
Genre:	**Folktale**
Level:	**Bridge; Intermediate (2–6)**
Elements:	**II. Places and Regions; IV. Human Systems; V. Environment and Society**
Themes:	**Place; Region; Human/Environment Interaction**

The Book

This beautifully illustrated traditional Buddhist jataka tale relates the story of a beneficent monkey king. A group of monkeys lived in a very special tree high on a mountain alongside a river. This tree bore delicious and fragrant fruit. The monkey king and his subjects tried to protect the fruit from greedy humans. One day, when a selfish human king found the tree, the monkeys were put in peril. The monkey king risked his life to save the other monkeys. So impressed was the human king that he spared the monkey king's life and adopted his lesson of generosity.

 # *Once a Mouse . . .*

Projection:	*Once a Mouse . . .* **retold by Marcia Brown, 1961**
Genre:	**Fable**
Level:	**Primary (K–2)**
Elements:	**II. Places and Regions; IV. Human Systems**
Themes:	**Location; Place; Human/Environment Interaction**

The Book

This fable presents the moral that pride goes before a fall. A hermit saved a little frightened mouse from being eaten by a crow and decided to keep it. When a cat stalked the mouse, the hermit magically changed the mouse into a bigger, ferocious cat. Every time a bigger animal threatened his pet, the hermit changed the mouse into a larger animal. Finally the mouse was turned into a huge royal tiger who strutted proudly through the jungle. Although warned by the hermit that such pride was not good, the angry tiger decided to kill his former protector. The hermit foiled the plan, and the tiger was changed back into a mouse who had to survive in the jungle on his own.

The Stone Cutter

Projection:	*The Stone Cutter* retold by Pam Newton, 1990
Genre:	Folktale
Level:	Bridge (2–4)
Elements:	II. Places and Regions; III. Physical Systems; V. Environment and Society
Themes:	Place; Region; Human/Environment Interaction

The Book

This Indian folktale tells of a poor stone cutter who was very unhappy with his lot in life. He prayed to the stone spirit to make him a rich man, for that would truly make him happy. Although the spirit granted the wish, the stone cutter's happiness was short-lived when he saw the wealth of the king. Once again the spirit granted his wish. The stone cutter was never satisfied for long, for he prayed for and became, in turn, the sun, cloud, wind, and mountain. His final wish was to be turned back to a stone cutter. Now he was truly a happy man.

Realm References

Bannerman, H., and F. Marcellino. 1996. *The Story of Little Babaji*. New York: HarperCollins.

Bash, B. 1996. *In the Heart of the Village*. San Francisco, CA: Sierra Club Books for Children.

Brown, M. 1961. *Once a Mouse . . .* . New York: Aladdin Books.

Demi. 1996. *Buddha*. New York: Henry Holt.

Margolies, B. A. 1992. *Kanu of Kathmandu: A Journey in Nepal*. New York: Four Winds Press.

Martin, R. 1997. *The Monkey Bridge*. New York: Alfred A. Knopf.

Newton, P. 1990. *The Stone Cutter*. New York: G. P. Putnam's Sons.

Staples, S. F. 1989. *Shabanu: Daughter of the Wind*. New York: Alfred A. Knopf.

Chapter 9
East Asian Realm

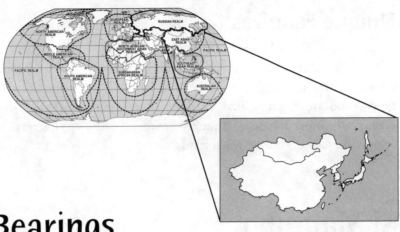

 Getting Your Bearings

Location

The East Asian Realm, located in the Eastern Hemisphere, is the most populous of the twelve realms. It has China at its center, with over a billion people. It also includes Japan, a densely populated five-island country considered a world economic power. There are four other political components: Mongolia, North Korea, South Korea, and Taiwan. Beijing is the capital city of China, the largest nation in this realm, and Tokyo is the capital of Japan. In addition, Hong Kong reunified with China in 1997, and Macao will be assimilated in 1999. East Asia is expansive, lying between 54°N and 18°N latitude, and 78°E and 145°E longitude.

Topography

This realm includes vast desert areas, including the Gobi Desert; the highest mountains in the world (the Himalayas); the Plateau of Tibet; and a multitude of islands, including Japan and Taiwan. The Manchurian and North China Plains are the major flat lands. In addition, the two major rivers of the realm are located in China, the Huang (Yellow) and the Yangtze. The flat areas of Japan are located in four small plains in the district of Hokkaido, where the population is the densest. The remaining 71 percent of the land is extremely mountainous, with Mount Fuji being the tallest peak at 12,388 feet.

Climate

This very large realm runs the spectrum of climatic conditions, ranging from arid and semiarid desert to humid temperate climates, from cold northern polar regions to steamy tropics. An alpine climate prevails in the highland areas of the Himalayas. Rainfall is heavier in the southern and central areas of China than in Mongolia. Monsoons are common in the coastal areas, bringing heavy summer rainfall. Although the climate varies from north to south, Japan is generally a humid oceanic climate influenced by the monsoons. This humidity brings heavy snows in the north during the winter and ample rainfall during the summer months throughout the islands. The mountains provide a respite from the summer heat in the low-lying populous areas.

Flora and Fauna

There is a variety of animal and bird life throughout this expansive realm. The most notable animals in the southwest corner of China are the great panda, the red panda, the golden-haired monkey, and the musk deer. Tigers, antelopes, leopards, and moose as well as wild horses are found in the northeast. The yak, the sand grouse, and the snow cock are common in Tibet. In the north of Japan is the unique Japanese macaque, a small monkey. In China, fir and broadleaf forests occur in the mountainous west. Bamboo, a favorite food of the giant panda, grows in many areas of the realm.

Unique Features

Cultural features include a variety of ethnic groups such as the Mongols, Turks, Uygurs, and Tajiks—who are Eurasian—and Korean, Japanese, and Chinese—who are Asian. China, in the center of the realm, is the most populous nation in the world, with approximately 1.3 billion inhabitants.

Japan is very densely populated, 321 persons per square kilometer, making it seventh in the world for population density. Japanese is the spoken language, but the written language is derived from Chinese characters. The population is 99.4 percent Japanese.

 # Mapping

 # *Huan Ching and the Golden Fish*

Projection:	*Huan Ching and the Golden Fish* by Michael Reeser, 1993
Genre:	Picture Storybook
Level:	Primary (K–2)
Elements:	I. The World in Spatial Terms; II. Places and Regions; IV. Human Systems
Themes:	Location; Place; Region

The Book

Huan Ching worked many months constructing and painting a five-foot-long kite in the shape of a goldfish to enter in the beautiful kite contest and the kite war competition on *Chung Yang Chieh* (kite-flying holiday). There were many brightly colored paper and silk kites of different types, such as bats and butterflies. Huan's kite looked like a beautiful goldfish swimming in the air, and it was chosen best kite.

In the kite war, Huan tried to cut the other kite strings with his kite string as the kites were floating in the air. Huan beat all competitors and made the final competition. Although he tried his best, Huan finally lost the kite war to his father. The holiday ended with a great feast on the mountain.

Key Understandings

Each culture develops traditional activities related to holiday celebrations, such as the kite-flying holiday of *Chung Yang Chieh* in the Chinese culture.

Knowledge

- Identify the symbolism of kites in Chinese culture.
- Describe the topography necessary for the flying of kites as it relates to the story.
- Compare and contrast the kites made in Huan Ching's culture to those of American culture.

Skills

- Ask questions about the construction and symbolism of kites in China.

- Find information in trade books.
- Organize and compare the information according to symbols and models.
- Draw conclusions concerning the importance of kites in the Chinese culture as compared to American culture.

Perspectives

Recognize and prize the similarities of customs among cultures.

Activities

I = Individual   P = Pairs   G = Group

A. FLYING OVER HUAN CHING'S WORLD (G)

Materials: student atlas, wall map of China, inflatable globe, string, tape, scissors, outline map of China, crayons

Students should locate China and the United States on the globe. Using string, tape one end in the center of China and cut the other end to fit in the students' home state. Take the wall map and place it on the floor. Students should sit in a circle around the map while holding the student atlas open to the map of China. Each student is to follow the outline of China by hand on the floor map as well as in the atlas. Using the outline map and their crayons, students trace the map of China, color the interior, and print the name of the country.

Questions to Ask

1. On the globe, is China close to or far from the United States?
2. Using your string as the route to China, what would you have to cross to get there?
3. After tracing and coloring China, what shapes come to mind?
4. Is the shape of China similar to or different from the United States?

B. FLYING FISH (G)

Materials: variety of colored tissue paper, white glue, glue sticks, colorful ribbons, glitter, aluminum wire, string, large paper clip, poster-board fish patterns, scissors

Have each group of students select two sheets of colorful tissue paper and place them on tables. Place the fish pattern on the paper and trace. Cut out the fish. Using the white glue on the outside edge of the fish, attach the two sides together. Leave the mouth area free of glue. Let dry overnight. Decorate the fish with glitter, using glue sticks. Make features such as eyes and gills out of different-colored tissue papers. Add ribbons of various lengths and colors by gluing to the bottom of the fish. Take the thin, flexible wire and shape a circle, twisting the ends closed. Glue the wire in the mouth, flapping the tissue inside so as to hide the wire. (This step requires teacher assistance.) Punch a hole anywhere near the edge of the fish. Use the paper clip as a hook through the punched hole and tie the string to the other end. Hang the fish kites throughout the room.

Fish kites a-making.

c. KITE HOLIDAY FEAST (CHUNG YANG CHIEH) (I)

Materials: lined paper, pencils, construction paper, scissors, crayons, patterns (butterfly, owl, chicken, dragon, fish), clear contact paper, fortune cookies, egg rolls, wonton chips, paper plates, napkins

Students write a short note inviting parents to the *Chung Yang Chieh*. They may decorate the invitations with a variety of kites. The teacher should invite parents to bring the suggested food items.

Choose a pattern and trace it on the construction paper. Cut out the figures after coloring and decorating both sides. Teacher covers fronts and backs of the place mats with clear contact paper. Put the place mats on the tables in preparation for the feast. Students and parents celebrate the holiday by eating and conversing under the colorful kites from "Flying Fish."

The Great Wall of China

Projection:	*The Great Wall of China* by Leonard Everett Fisher, 1986
Genre:	Historical Fiction
Level:	Intermediate (4–6)
Elements:	I. The World in Spatial Terms; II. Places and Regions; IV. Human Systems
Themes:	Location; Place; Movement

The Book

Around 200 B.C., the first supreme emperor of China wanted to stop the barbarous Mongols from the north from invading China. The way to do this, he decided, was to repair and connect the old walls together and build one long wall across the top of China. It would stand five men high and wide enough to hold ten soldiers side by side. The wall would have two-story watchtowers built every hundred yards for sighting any invaders.

An army of a million forced laborers, working day and night for ten years under terrible conditions, completed the monumental task. The Great Wall of China spanned over a thousand miles, forming a boundary of safety for the country.

Great human suffering and toil contributed to the construction of one of the greatest engineering feats and most successful protective barriers in the world for that time.

Knowledge

- Identify the regions through which the Great Wall of China was built.
- Describe the topography over which the Great Wall was constructed.
- Compare and contrast the Great Wall to other remarkable engineering feats around the world.
- State the reasons why the Great Wall was significant to the first supreme emperor and the people of China.

Skills

- Ask questions about the construction and location of the Great Wall.
- Collect information from a variety of sources.
- Compile and analyze information relative to the achievement and significance of building the Great Wall.

Key Understandings

The Chinese, like all people, wanted to protect themselves from conflict and control their own lands; thus, the Great Wall of China was constructed to help the emperor protect his people from the barbarous Mongol invaders.

- Draw conclusions about the effectiveness of the Great Wall as a deterrent to aggressors.

Perspectives

Value the sacrifices of hundreds of thousands of people to bring order and protection to their lives. Appreciate the monumental accomplishments of the Chinese people.

Activities

I = Individual   P = Pairs   G = Group

A. PLOTTING THE GREAT WALL (I, P, G)

Materials: student atlas, globe, map on pp. 4–5 of *The Great Wall of China*, outline map of China, markers, pencils, crayons

On the outline map of China, students plot the location and the extent of the Great Wall. Label the major rivers and land forms along the wall. Identify any cities that lie in reasonable proximity to the wall, including the ancient and modern capitals of China. Place a scale of miles and a title on the map.

Questions to Ask

1. Where is the northernmost point of the Great Wall located? southernmost? easternmost? westernmost?
2. Through what rivers and land forms does the Great Wall pass? What rivers and land forms lie nearby?
3. How many miles long, from start to finish, is the Great Wall?
4. Why did the emperor choose this location?
5. Using what you know about this structure, why do you think it was so effective?

B. THE SEVEN WONDERS (P, G)

Materials: information books, *National Geographic*, travel magazines and brochures, poster board, pencils, white glue, scissors, markers

Students gather information on the seven human-made wonders of the world. They should also find illustrations that can be cut out or copied and cut out. On the poster board, draw a comparison matrix with each of the wonders listed across the top and factors such as time frame, materials, purpose, durability, location, and size listed down the left side. Decorate with pictures of the wonders across the top as well. Fill in the boxes with the appropriate information. Based on the information, evaluate the relative amount of effort taken to construct each wonder and formulate conclusions about which one constitutes the most important achievement. Students must provide a rationale for their conclusions. Compile this information into a final report and attach it to the poster. Title the final product.

C. CHOPS AND CULTURE (I)

Materials: writing paper, pencils, potatoes, red ink pad, paring knives, potato peeler, digging tools (e.g., awl)

Have students design chops (seals) that include their initials. Develop meaningful symbols and arrange them to form another chop. When the designs are finished, the students should carve them into halved potatoes. Using a red ink pad, ink the carved surface of the potato end and stamp on writing paper. Write paragraphs about the significance of the designs. Have students pair up and share their paragraphs and chops. Display the finished products around the room for all to view.

 # Crow Boy

Projection:	*Crow Boy* by Taro Yashima, 1983
Genre:	Picture Storybook
Level:	Primary (K–2)
Element:	I. The World in Spatial Terms; II. Places and Regions
Themes:	Location; Place

The Book

Chibi, which means "tiny boy" in Japanese, was a shy boy shunned by his classmates in the village school. He was frightened of other people, and this attitude made him misunderstood by his teachers and his peers. He left alone during school and play time. During his first five years of school, Chibi found solace in the environment around him, particularly by observing the sounds and sights of the animals, especially the crows.

When Chibi was in the sixth grade, Mr. Isobe, the new teacher, gave Chibi confidence to enter a talent show to present his special skill—imitating the different voices of crows. His schoolmates were amazed at his ability to imitate the variety of crow calls that he had learned while he walked from his home in the country at dawn and returned at sunset every day for six years. From this time on, no one in the village called him Chibi; instead they called him Crow Boy.

Key Understandings

The environment influences relationships among individuals. Observation and interaction with the flora and fauna of a region can play a role in these relationships.

Knowledge

- Identify the realm and region, noting the climate, flora, and fauna.
- Describe the major character's cultural environment (language, clothing, foods).
- Articulate a mental map of Crow Boy's route to school as well as the students' own routes.
- Compare and contrast the region and the physical and cultural environment with the students' own.

Skills

- Gather illustrated geographic information about characteristics of the location and culture of Chibi's environment.
- Organize and classify the collected geographic information.
- Analyze the role of environment and its impact upon human behavior.

Perspectives

Value the varieties of nature and their influence upon a person's life.

Activities

I = Individual   P = Pairs   G = Group

A. LOCATING CROW BOY'S WORLD (P)

Materials: relief globe, string

Using a relief globe, determine the realm and region of the student's personal location and Chibi's location. Tie a string to the student's finger. Use that finger to point to personal location. Then extend the other end of the string to Chibi's location, noting the distance and land and water forms between the two.

Questions to Ask

1. Is Crow Boy's country larger or smaller than your country?
2. Is Japan on the same or the opposite side of the globe as your country?
3. The color for water on a globe is blue: Which country is surrounded by water?

4. If an island is land surrounded by water, is your country an island country? Is Japan an island country?

5. About how many islands make up the island country of Japan?

6. Since the story does not tell where Crow Boy lived, choose an island on which he might have lived. Can you feel the mountainous and flat areas on that island?

B. MAPPING WALK (I, P, G)

Materials: sneakers, good weather, neighborhood trail or school path, reproducible map, crayons, pencil

Listen carefully to the description of Chibi's walk to and from school. Create a mental map of his walk. Then describe the physical features (e.g., trees, hills) and flora and fauna that Chibi would have observed and heard. Draw the symbols for the key items on the reproducible map (see Figure 9.1 on page 109). Choose two of your own to add to the key. On the route, draw the symbols for what Crow Boy would have seen on his way.

On a walk look and listen carefully to the sights and sounds of this environment. Listen and attempt to imitate, as Chibi did, the calls of birds or animals. Using the same symbols from Crow Boy's map, draw the symbols on the map for your walk to and from school on the reproducible (see Figure 9.2 on page 110).

C. KAMISHIBAI THEATER (P, G)

Materials: cardboard box, ruler, pencil, X-Acto knife, tape, crayons, watercolors, magazine pictures, white glue or paste, poster board or tag board, scissors

This traditional storytelling presentation uses a small box theater and story cards. Presenters slide appropriately decorated story cards through the slots on either side of the box theater. While this is being done, the presenter tells a story that focuses on the pictures drawn on the story cards.

1. **Making the theater (teacher/parent task)**

Select a cardboard box of any size (medium size is recommended). Place box on its bottom so that either longer side is exposed. Starting 1 inch from the side and ending 1 inch from the opposite side, draw a horizontal line 1 to 2 inches parallel to the top and the bottom of the box. Now draw a vertical line from the midpoint of the top horizontal line to the bottom line. Using an X-Acto knife, carefully cut on the drawn lines. Using a straight edge as a guide, fold back the flaps to create the doors of the stage. To make vertical slots on the smaller sides of the box, draw a vertical line parallel to the stage, beginning and ending 1 inch from the top and bottom edges of the box. Draw another parallel line 2 inches above the first vertical line. Connect the lines. Following these lines, cut out a slot. Repeat this procedure on the opposite side. Close and tape the top and the bottom of the box. Decorate the theater box (student task). The box may be decorated using various materials (i.e., watercolors, wallpaper, pictures).

2. **Making the story cards (teacher/parent with student)**

Based on the length of the slot and the width of the box, cut four story cards from poster board or tagboard so they can be slid through the slots made and so they extend 2 inches beyond the theater box on both sides. Number each card on the back with the numbers 1–4 (student task). Card 1: Print CHIBI'S MAP STORY. Card 2: Based on the island that you chose as a possible home location for Chibi, draw the physical features, including the flora and fauna that Chibi observed during his walk to and from school. Make sure to decorate the entire card. Card 3: Print MY MAP STORY. Card 4: Draw the physical features, including the flora and fauna, that you observed on your walk. On the right-hand side of the back of this story card, write two or three key words to remind the presenter of the important parts of the story for cards 2 and 4.

3. **Making the presentation (student task)**
   Place the four cards in order in the slots. Card 1: Introduce the title, telling the audience the name of the picture storybook from which it came. With your right hand, slide the title card out of the theater. Card 2: Tell the story of Chibi's walk, mapping out the sights and sounds along the way. This would be a good time to imitate the crow calls and other sounds. Slide the card through the right slot. Card 3: Introduce your mapping story, telling the location of your own walk. Slide the card through the slot. Card 4: Tell the story of your own walk, mapping out the sights and sounds along the way.

D. SCHOOL CULTURE (I, P, G)

Materials: white rice (minute or boiling bag), water, chopsticks, fork, small bowls, napkins, green leaf (spinach, lettuce, or radish), stove top or other cooking facility

View the illustrations in the book. Search for information using these questions as a guide: What does the classroom look like? Do the students use desks? Chalkboards? What kind of games are they playing? How do the children dress? What foods do they have for lunch? How do they write their letters? List the similarities and differences between Chibi's school and your school.

After noting the differences between writing styles, print the words for *rice* and *friendship* in your style. Copy the symbols for *rice* and *friendship* in Japanese picture writing.

Using plain cooked white rice in individual bowls, try eating with chopsticks. Repeat this activity using a fork.

1. Was eating with chopsticks an easy task?
2. Did many grains of rice make it to your mouth? Did you finish eating all of the rice?
3. Was eating with the fork easier than eating with chopsticks?
4. Give reasons for your choice.

Now, place a tablespoon of rice in a washed green leaf (spinach, lettuce, or radish) and roll it into a ball, a rice ball. Enjoy lunch as Chibi did.

The Magic Fan

Projection:	*The Magic Fan* by Keith Baker, 1989
Genre:	Picture Storybook
Level:	Intermediate (4–6)
Elements:	I. The World in Spatial Terms; III. Physical Systems; V. Environment and Society; VI. The Uses of Geography
Themes:	Place; Region; Human/Environment Interaction

The Book

Colorful fans illustrate this story. To enhance the plot, fan flaps are used to distinguish before and after situations. The fans depict the story of Yoshi, who lived by the sea and loved to build everything the villagers needed. One night, as he sat looking at the sea, a magic fan floated toward him. Yoshi opened the fan

to new building adventures: a boat to sail the sea; a kite to fly to the sky; and a bridge to stretch across his village. The villagers were angry because the bridge cast a dark shadow, so Yoshi began to cut it down when an earthquake caused it to shake and tremble. Yoshi urged the villagers to seek safety on the bridge, for a tsunami (tidal wave) would soon destroy the village. The people on the bridge were saved. Despite the loss of his magic fan during the storm, Yoshi knew what he must do. He led the villagers in building a new, beautiful village. He discovered that without the fan, the magic was his own.

Key Understandings

Interacting with the forces of nature, such as the sea, affects the environment and the lives of the people in it.

Knowledge

- Identify the realm and region, noting island features, bodies of water, tectonic plates, and fault-line boundaries.
- Describe the major characteristics of abodes and other structures by the sea.
- Describe the interdependence of the villagers when rebuilding their community.
- Compare and contrast the physical features of this region to the western United States, including frequency of earthquakes, fault-line boundaries, bodies of water, and the like.

Skills

- Formulate a list of questions related to earthquakes and tidal waves, especially those that affect Japan.
- Gather and organize information concerning earthquakes and tidal waves, using library and/or Internet sources.
- Analyze the impact of earthquakes and tidal waves on Japan as well as on Yoshi's village, including positive and negative consequences.

Perspectives

Believe in the importance of preparing for nature's disasters.

Activities

I = Individual   P = Pairs   G = Group

A. PLOTTING YOSHI'S REGION (P)

Materials: geopolitical globe, world map of fault lines and plate tectonics

Using a globe with lines of latitude and longitude, locate and name the lines that border the north, south, east, and west of Japan. Repeat the same process with California and the students' home state. Using the map of fault lines and plates, again locate Japan, California, and the home state. Record the degrees of latitude and longitude surrounding each location and the name of the applicable plate and nearest fault line.

Questions to Ask

1. How do the latitude and longitude of Japan compare to the other two sites?
2. What are the names of the plates upon which each site is located?
3. Based on its location, which site would be most likely to have a tsunami after an earthquake?
4. Why would Yoshi's village be more exposed to a tsunami?
5. In which area would you prefer to live? Explain why.

B. INVENTING A TSUNAMI-SAFE CITY (G, P)

Materials: butcher paper, tape, white glue, marking pens, pencils, crayons, any materials appropriate for specific structures

Invention, as used here, is the process of developing a better way to build structures to withstand the effects of a tsunami. Students should be provided opportunities to create a model structure that meets specific criteria formulated from research on the nature of the location and natural forces. The Tsunami-safe City should be divided into sections, with each group taking responsibility for the structures in its section. When each section is completed, the students will organize a display of the Tsunami-safe City.

Structure Schema

Identify and state the purpose of the structure to be built. List the criteria that your structure should meet. Sketch a model of the intended outcome.

Structure Construction

Gather materials appropriate to the model. Begin construction, keeping in mind that alternative plans may be necessary to meet the structure's standards. At various stages in the construction, students should step back and reflect on their progress. Students should be encouraged to constantly search for improvements in the model. When the criteria have been met, the building of the section is completed.

Structure Evaluation

Have students determine whether the criteria were clearly stated. Was the model distinct enough for the students to follow to accurately build the structure? Have the students decide whether the reflection process resulted in an improved structure. Discover the extent to which the established criteria have been met.

Structure the City

On a paper-covered flat surface, the students should come to consensus as to the placement of each structure in the city. Add the ocean, trees, streets, and the other features, to make the city complete. Name the city and place a compass rose on this newly created city map.

Chibi: A True Story from Japan

Projection:	*Chibi: A True Story from Japan* by Barbara Benner and Julia Takaya, 1996
Genre:	Fiction; Chapter Book
Level:	Bridge; Intermediate (2–6)
Elements:	I. The World in Spatial Terms; II. Places and Regions; V. Environment and Society; VI. The Uses of Geography
Themes:	Location; Place; Human/Environment Interaction

The Book

Flying over the skyscrapers of Tokyo, a mother duck, an *oka-san kamo,* spied a pool of water in an office park that would be a perfect home for her future family. She set up a nest near the pool, and soon nine of the ten eggs hatched. Finally the tenth one cracked open, revealing the tiniest family member, Chibi.

When the *oka-san* walked her ducklings, office workers, families, and television reporters came to watch them. Being the tiniest, Chibi became the favorite. Oka-san chose a new home across the highway for her growing brood. With the help of Sato-san, who stopped traffic so the ducks could safely cross, the family settled in the moat of the Imperial Gardens.

A typhoon hit Tokyo, and when it cleared, the duck watchers discovered that Chibi was missing! While searching the moat, Sato-san found Chibi on a floating plastic-foam plate. Chibi's return was news throughout Tokyo.

Because of the concern for the now famous duck family, the emperor had a special strong duck house built for them in the moat. This is a true story.

Key Understandings

People in a society need to provide for the survival of wildlife, not only for present but for future generations. The interactions between individuals and wildlife add to the beauty and enjoyment of life.

Knowledge

- Identify the region of the story.
- Describe the cultural geography of the city of Tokyo.

- Describe the interdependence of city people with the ducks.
- Explain the characteristics of the natural habitat and lifestyle of wild ducks.
- Describe the cause and effects of a typhoon.

Skills

- Develop a list of questions relating to duck habitat. Using the list as a framework, gather information and pictures from appropriate sources.
- Organize the duck habitat information into categories: environment, food, climate, and so on.
- Analyze the advantages and disadvantages of natural and human-made habitats for ducks.
- Answer the geographic questions by creating various forms (e.g., maps, models, articles).

Perspectives

Appreciate the benefits of wildlife preservation to society.

Activities

I = Individual   P = Pairs   G = Group

A. VIEWING CHIBI'S HABITAT (P)

Materials: satellite image of Tokyo, geopolitical map of Honshú, city map of Tokyo, drawing paper, crayons, markers, pencil, ruler

Using a map of Japan, locate the island of Honshú. On a satellite image of Tokyo, locate possible safe habitats for Chibi and his family. Compare the satellite image to a map of Tokyo displaying notable sites (parks, buildings, etc.). Go to the library media center and gather, organize, and categorize information on ducks and their habitats. From information gathered, create a map from a bird's-eye view (duck's-eye view), noting both physical and cultural symbols

of the perfect habitat for the positive interaction between humans and ducks in Tokyo.

Questions to Ask

1. What major cities are located on the island of Honshú? Which one is the capital?
2. What physical features (rivers, bay, lakes, parks) do you see on the satellite image of Tokyo? Can you locate these on the map?
3. Based on all of the information gathered, what things need to be available to sustain Chibi and his family?
4. Where in Tokyo can you find possible sites for Chibi to live? Which site do you think is best?
5. How does your map compare with the Tokyo site selected as the best for Chibi?
6. How does your design provide for the safe interaction between humans and ducks?
7. Are there any places in your own area that would be a good sanctuary for this wild duck family? Explain.

B. DUCK-WATCH REPORTER (I)

Materials: computer, printer, paper

Create a headline and front-page story about the adventures of Chibi and the duck family following the typhoon. The headline of the story must include a reference to the typhoon that hit Tokyo. For the story itself, information about the cause and destructive power of the typhoon as well as the experience of the Tokyo citizens and the duck family should be researched and presented.

Draw pictures to accompany the story. These pictures should represent the actual devastation produced by a typhoon. Use of research information should be evident in these pictures.

Data, including photographic, concerning typhoons and their devastation should be researched in the school or public library before beginning this project. This research should support information noted in the newspaper story. Compile stories into a newsbook for display for others to read.

c. Duck House (G)

Materials: construction materials based on design (e.g., balsa wood, plastic-foam trays, Popsicle-type sticks, cardboard, paint, "duck" tape, glue)

Based on typhoon data gathered in "Duck-watch Reporter" and duck research from "Viewing Chibi's Habitat," construct a workable floating model for a house that would be appropriate for Chibi and his family. Use the picture in the book to determine necessary features. Students should be creative in their designs. Test the model in an appropriate water container.

Figure 9.1–Crow Boy's Map

Map Key

TREE

LAKE

RIVER

ROAD

BRIDGE

HILLS

HOUSE

Figure 9.2—My Map

Map Key

TREE

LAKE

RIVER

ROAD

BRIDGE

HILLS

HOUSE

Charting with More Books

 ## *Peacebound Trains*

Projection:	*Peacebound Trains* by Haemi Balgassi, 1996
Genre:	Fiction; Chapter Book
Level:	Intermediate (4–6)
Elements:	I. The World in Spatial Terms; II. Places and Regions; IV. Human Systems
Themes:	Location; Place; Movement

The Book

Sumi lived with her grandmother, Harmuny, while her mother completed her training as a soldier. Harmuny told her of the happy days many years ago before the war with the North, when she lived happily in Seoul with her husband, Harabujy, and her two children.

Harmuny and her family were forced to leave their home and began their harrowing journey south. After walking for several days along with other refugees, they came upon a train that was going to Pusan, their last chance to get to safety. After Harabujy found a place on the roof of a train car for Harmuny and the children, he told her that he had to remain to fight for his country. That was the last time Harmuny was to see him.

Sumi knew that, unlike her grandmother, whose train took her away from the person she loved, someday soon the train would bring Sumi's mother safely to her.

 ## *Dragon Kite of the Autumn Moon*

Projection:	*Dragon Kite of the Autumn Moon* by Valerie Reddix, 1991
Genre:	Picture Storybook
Level:	Bridge; Intermediate (2–6)
Element:	I. The World in Spatial Terms; II. Places and Regions
Themes:	Location; Place

The Book

Ever since he could remember, Tad-Tin, a young Taiwanese boy, and his grandfather had made a special kite for Kite's Day. They would fly it all day until dark. Then, following an ancient Chinese tradition, Grandfather would cut the string so that the kite would carry away all their misfortunes. This year Grandfather was ill and could not join him. Tad-Tin decided to fly the huge dragon kite that Grandfather had made to celebrate his birth.

When it became dark, he lit the green lanterns that were used for the dragon's eyes and flew the kite. He let the string go. When he returned to the house, he found Grandfather feeling better. The magic dragon kite had taken away their misfortune.

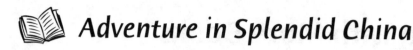 Adventure in Splendid China

Projection:	*Adventure in Splendid China* by Erika Fabian, 1993
Genre:	Picture Storybook; Information Book
Level:	Intermediate (4-6)
Elements:	I. The World in Spatial Terms; II. Places and Regions; IV. Human Systems
Themes:	Location; Place; Region

The Book

Through a blend of fantasy in the drawings and information in the text and photos, this story tells of the adventure of five children led by the monkey god of China. This legendary creature took the children through magical means, such as riding a flying dragon kite, to visit theme parks throughout China. They were introduced to a variety of tales, customs, crafts, abodes, music, and dances special to the regions. At each place they were given a gift unique to the region, such as silk welcoming scarves from Mongolia.

The Warrior and the Wise Man

Projection:	*The Warrior and the Wise Man* by David Wisniewski, 1989
Genre:	Picture Storybook
Level:	Intermediate (4-6)
Elements:	I. The World in Spatial Terms; III. Physical Systems; V. Environment and Society
Themes:	Location; Human/Environment Interaction

The Book

In ancient Japan, Tozaemon and Toemon, twin sons of the emperor, may have looked alike but possessed very different personalities. As a test to determine which one would take the throne, the emperor sent them on a mission to gather the five eternal elements in order to overcome the demons of earth, fire, wind, water, and cloud. Toemon called upon his skills as a warrior, angered the demons, and thus failed to collect the elements, while Tozaemon pursued the five eternal elements using his wit and wisdom. The result was that wisdom won over ferocity and the wise Tozaemon proved to be better suited to become emperor.

Grandfather's Journey

Projection: *Grandfather's Journey* by Allen Say, 1993
Genre: Picture Storybook
Level: Intermediate (4–6)
Elements: I. The World in Spatial Terms; II. Places and Regions; IV. Human Systems
Themes: Location; Place; Movement; Human/Environment Interaction

The Book

A grandson relates the travels of his grandfather as a young man from Japan to California, where he was introduced to the different topography and culture of a new country. He returned home, married his sweetheart, and brought her back to California, where they raised their daughter in a new culture.

Years later, longing for the mountains and rivers of his former home, the grandfather returned with his family to Japan. The grandson, having heard stories of California, made many journeys between Japan and the United States and, like his grandfather, came to love both.

Realm References

Baker, K. 1989. *The Magic Fan*. San Diego, CA: Harcourt Brace.

Balgassi, H. 1996. *Peacebound Trains*. New York: Clarion Books.

Brenner, B., and J. Takaya. 1996. *Chibi: A True Story from Japan*. New York: Clarion Books.

Fabian, E. 1993. *Adventure in Splendid China*. San Francisco, CA: Getherease.

Fisher, L. E. 1986. *The Great Wall of China*. New York: Macmillan.

Reddix, V. 1991. *Dragon Kite of the Autumn Moon*. New York: Lothrop, Lee and Shepard Books.

Reeser, M. 1993. *Huan Ching and the Golden Fish*. Austin, TX: Steck-Vaughn.

Say, A. 1993. *Grandfather's Journey*. Boston, MA: Houghton Mifflin.

Wisniewski, D. 1989. *The Warrior and the Wise Man*. New York: Lothrop, Lee and Shepard Books.

Yashima, T. 1983. *Crow Boy*. New York: Viking Penguin.

Chapter 10
Southeast Asian Realm

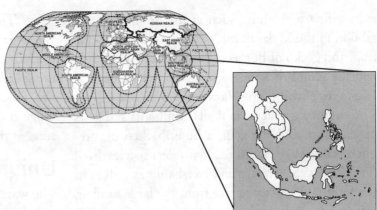

 Getting Your Bearings

Location

Bordered on the north by China and the west by India, this realm consists of islands and peninsulas. The mainland peninsula of the realm is bordered by the Bay of Bengal, on the west, the South China Sea on the south and east, and China on the north. Mainland countries include Myanmar (formerly Burma), Thailand, Malaysia, Cambodia, Vietnam, and landlocked Laos. The island nations, surrounded by the Indian Ocean on the west and the Pacific Ocean on the east are Indonesia, Brunei, the Philippines, and the offshore part of Malaysia. Singapore, one of the most densely populated countries in the world, is an island nation found off the tip of mainland Malaysia. This realm covers 1,636,537 square miles with Indonesia, the world's largest archipelago, being the largest nation. Major cities in the realm, in descending order of population, include Jakarta, Indonesia; Bangkok, Thailand; Manila, Philippines; Ho Chi Minh City, South Vietnam; and Yangon (formerly Rangoon), Myanmar.

Topography

The Southeast Asian Realm consists of over 20,000 islands and a peninsular mainland with beautiful beaches, rugged shoreline, and far-flung islands. Several mountain ranges, including the Dawna and Bilauktaung Ranges in Thailand and Myanmar, are characteristic of both the islands and peninsula areas. The highest mountain in the islands, Kinabalu at 13,455 feet in the Crocker Range, rises on the island of Borneo in East Malaysia. On the peninsula in Myanmar, Mount Hkakabo at 19,290 feet is the highest point in the realm. Active volcanoes are commonplace, with Krakatau in Indonesia and Mount Pinatubo in the Philippines being the most well-known. Two major rivers are the Irrawaddy and the Mekong, running through the peninsula areas and forming large, productive deltas as they reach, respectively, the Bay of Bengal and the South China Sea.

Climate

Because the equator cuts through this realm, the climate is tropical, warm, and humid throughout the year. The monsoons provide two seasons, dry and wet, for Myanmar, Thailand, Cambodia, Laos, and Vietnam. The monsoons dispense an equal amount of rain in Indonesia and the southern coastal areas of Vietnam and the Malay Peninsula. The Philippines are vulnerable to violent tropical storms called typhoons. High temperatures ranging from the mid-80s to the mid-90s, high rainfall averaging 118 inches to as much as 225 inches, and the resultant humidity characterize the realm. In the mountain areas, rain is the heaviest: Mount Kinabalu receives more than 30 feet of rain per year.

Flora and Fauna

The tropical climate supports rain forests rich in fabulous plant and animal life. The forests of the Indochinese Peninsula, Malaysia, the Philippines, and Indonesia are luxurious as well as fragile. Among the many forms of animal life found here are many extraordinary creatures such as the orangutan and gibbon in the Malayan forests and the flying snake, frog, and gecko of Borneo. On the Malay Peninsula and the island of Sumatra, the Asian elephant and two types of rhinoceros, Java and Sunda, are found. The kouprey, a wild ox, inhabits Cambodia and parts of Vietnam, and the gaur, a humpbacked ox, frequents the Malay Peninsula. Many deer species dwell on the grassy savannahs and riverbanks as well as in the forests; they vary in size from the large sambar, almost 5 feet tall, to the small mouse deer, 20 inches tall. Among the predatory animals, the tiger and leopard are most notable. Along the shores live giant sea turtles, loggerheads, and green turtles. In the mangrove swamps of southern Asia, aquatic species such as the archerfish and mudskipper are unique. The Komodo dragon of Komodo Island in Indonesia is an enormous reptile measuring up to 13 feet.

The tropical rain forest includes hundreds of species of flowering plants and a variety of trees, both hardwood and fruit-bearing. Indonesia has one of the greatest forest reserves in the world. Bamboo thickets and palm trees create a fascinating atmosphere for the forests. The rafflesia flower, famous for its offensive smell and large size, 3 feet across, is a rare rain-forest plant. Orchids and ferns grow in the mountain forests. Along the shoreline, the coconut palm tree is the dominant tree. Three types of unusually shaped mangroves—red, bruguiera, and sonneratia—spread throughout specific areas of the coastlines.

Unique Features

The water connection, with both sea and river valleys, is an important aspect of this realm. On the mainland people have settled in the river valleys. Farmers primarily grow rice on terraced land using river water to irrigate their crops. The larger cities, such as Yangon, Phnom Penh, Bangkok, and Ho Chi Minh City, have grown in these river valleys. In the islands, spread out across the ocean, the people have located along the shores, depending on the water for food and travel. Because this realm is fragmented into several islands and peninsulas, and because of its location on major trade routes, colonization and the resultant conflict have created an unstable political and economic environment for years.

 **Mapping**

 Dia's Story Cloth

Projection:	Dia's *Story Cloth* by Dia Cha, 1996
Genre:	**Information Book**
Level:	**Intermediate (4-6)**
Elements:	**I. The World in Spatial Terms; II. Places and Regions; IV. Human Systems**
Themes:	**Location; Place; Regions; Movement; Human/Environment Interaction**

The Book

The Hmong story cloth depicts, in map form, images showing the history of the Hmong, "the free people." Narrated in first person by the author, the text and the map detail the exodus of the Hmong from China to settlements in Burma and Laos. The narrative embroidery shows the effect of the war in Laos between communists and loyalists and Dia's dangerous escape to a refugee camp in Thailand. The map concludes with Dia and her family boarding a plane and flying to their new home in the United States. In addition to the map, enlarged story-cloth inserts allow the reader to focus on particular events.

The Hmong traditions of the embroidered story cloth, the batik process, and fine needle and straw work are explained in the book as well.

Key Understandings

Mapping is one way to record history. The Hmong people use story cloths to pictorially record and preserve events and places in their personal history. The search for freedom plays a role in the movement of peoples from one land to another.

Knowledge

- Identify the countries to which the Hmong migrated.
- Describe the environment and land forms of the Southeast Asian peninsula.
- Identify the important events in the lives of the Hmong people.
- Describe the tradition of the story cloth.
- Depict the connection between Dia's story-cloth map and the history of her ancestors and family.

Skills

- Ask questions about the location and countries of Southeast Asia.
- Develop a list of questions about the history of the Hmong people as shown in the story cloth.
- Ask questions about the construction of a traditional story cloth.
- Gather information from a variety of library and Internet sources.
- Organize and analyze information into a physical and political map, story-cloth historical map, and bulletin board.
- Formulate conclusions concerning the importance of recording life events in various forms.

Perspectives

Value the ability of the Hmong people to overcome hardships associated with their search for freedom.

Activities

I = Individual   P = Pairs   G = Group

A. HMONG MAP (I)

Materials: large drawing paper, construction paper in a variety of colors, scissors, white glue, pastels, thin black marker, atlas, pencils, encyclopedia, *National Geographic* (October 1988, January 1974)

On the drawing paper, create a freehand map of the Southeast Asian peninsula that includes the political boundaries and geographic features. Using the pastels, color the water areas blue and the land areas a light shade of cream or tan. Be sure to identify Laos with a lighter color since it is the primary location for the Hmong. Include symbols for any mountain areas. In the tradition of the story cloth, map the story of the Hmong people, using figures in traditional dress. Frame the "Hmong Map" with colored construction paper in the story-cloth manner, using a typical pattern.

Questions to Ask

1. What countries make up the peninsula of Southeast Asia? Of these, to which ones did the Hmong migrate?
2. Which countries border Laos? How is Laos different from any of the other countries of the peninsula?
3. What are the outstanding geographical features on your Hmong map?
4. Why do you think the Hmong people settled where they did? How did they adapt to their new environment?
5. How did the location in Laos create a problem for the Hmong?

B. FREEDOM HOLD: REFUGEE BULLETIN BOARD (G)

Materials: political map of the world, yarn, pushpins, paper, library research materials, computer and printer

The teacher should select four to five refugee camps around the world, including any still remaining in Thailand. Assign each group one of these camps to research. Groups should find out about the location, who the refugees are, why they are there, how long they have resided there, what their life is like, and so on. Each group must write a refugee report on the computer. Hang the political map of the world on a wall. Use pushpins and yarn to identify the location of each refugee camp. Extend the yarn outside the map edges and connect the reports to the related camps. Each group makes an oral report predicting the prospects for freedom for the refugees in its assigned refugee camp.

c. Class Story Cloth (I)

Materials: fabric glue, felt squares, scissors, variety of fabric and felt scraps, yarn, large plastic-foam board

Have each student investigate an event in his or her own personal history. Gather information from primary sources: parents, photographs, videotapes, and the like. Each student should select one event to map on an individual story square on felt. Encourage students to create a colorful design making use of as many materials as appropriate. The fabric glue is handy for "stitching" fabric to the felt squares. Have students share their personal histories with classmates. In order to create the story cloth, have students arrange and glue their squares onto the large plastic-foam board, leaving at least 2 inches around the edges for a decorative border. Cut felt squares into 2-inch-wide strips and glue around the outside of the story cloth. Choosing a geometric design, decorate with this design used for an appliqué on the border. Display the "Class Story Cloth" for everyone to see.

Hush! A Thai Lullaby

Projection:	*Hush! A Thai Lullaby* by Minfong Ho, 1996
Genre:	Picture Storybook
Level:	Primary (K–2)
Elements:	II. Places and Regions; III. Physical Systems
Themes:	Place; Region

The Book

This lullaby, written in verse and illustrated in the traditional Thai style, tells the story of the efforts of a mother to silence all sounds so her baby would sleep. The pictures reveal the houses and environment of Thailand, while the sounds are those of familiar animals that are indigenous to the region or commonly kept around the home. At the end, in an interesting twist of fate, the baby was awake and the mother slept.

Key Understandings

In all environments there are peculiar sounds that provide a thumbprint of the region and are valued by the inhabitants.

Knowledge

- Identify the sounds in the baby's Thai environment.
- Describe the animals shown in *Hush!*
- Compare sounds in the baby's environment and in the classroom and community environment.

Skills

- Ask questions about the sounds of the baby's Thai environment.
- Gather information by listening, imitating, and taping sounds.
- Organize sounds into human, animal, and nature categories.
- Formulate conclusions about sound similarities between the baby's environment and the students'

neighborhood. Determine which sounds are good sounds and which are bad.

Perspectives

Appreciate the relationship of sounds to a personal environment.

Activities

I = Individual   P = Pairs   G = Group

A. Mapping Baby's Sounds (I)

Materials: **primary globe, yarn, masking tape, drawing paper, crayons**

Using a globe, help students find Thailand and their own location and then tape one end of a piece of yarn to their location and extend the other end to Thailand, noting the distance. After reading the book, children should draw and color the origins of the sounds in the book: human, animal, and wind. Have the students recreate on their maps each of the sounds represented on their maps while the teacher records them.

Questions to Ask

1. Is Thailand near or far from your country?
2. What animals are in the baby's environment?
3. Whose human voice is heard? How is this different from the sound of the wind?
4. How do these sounds compare to sounds that you hear every day?

B. Familiar Neighborhood Sounds (P)

Materials: **neighborhood map, crayons**

The teacher will lead students on a listening walk around the school neighborhood. Tell the students to make a picture in their minds as they walk. Working in pairs, the students should identify the sounds with visual cues for the locations. Back in the classroom, the students will form mental maps of their walk of neighborhood sounds and share them orally with partners. A teacher-made neighborhood wall map will be used to record the locations of sounds identified by the students. Have students draw a picture of the source of each sound in the appropriate location on the neighborhood wall map. This map may be added to upon further investigation. Have students discuss which sounds they liked and disliked and tell why.

C. Listening to My Environment (I, G)

Materials: **small tape recorder, tape, reproducible sound category sheet**

Ask children to do short tape recordings of sounds in and around their homes and bring the tapes to school. As each tape is played, have the other children try to guess the sources of the sounds. Provide children with a sheet of paper that is divided into four categories: human, animal, mechanical, and other (see Figure 10.1 on page 122). For each sound on the students' own tapes, a picture should be drawn under the appropriate category. Have students determine which type of sound they heard the most, which ones were pleasant or unpleasant, and which ones were peculiar to their own environment in comparison to others.

Sweet Dried Apples: A Vietnamese Wartime Childhood

Projection: *Sweet Dried Apples: A Vietnamese Wartime Childhood* by Rosemary Breckler, 1996

Genre: **Picture Storybook**

Level: **Bridge (2–4)**

Elements: **I. The World in Spatial Terms; II. Places and Regions; IV. Human Systems**

Themes: **Location; Place; Region; Movement; Human/Environment Interaction**

The Book

Based on a true story, a segment of the Vietnam War is described through the eyes of a young girl whose father, Ba, had joined the soldiers. Her grandfather, Ong Noi, came to take care of the family until her father returned. The young girl and her brother, Duc, could not resist the sweet dried apples that Ong Noi brought to add to his herbal remedies. The children spent many enjoyable hours with their grandfather, but the war continued to creep closer to the village. One night Ong Noi with his herbal remedies left to help the soldiers. During the many weeks that he was gone, the children collected herbs from the woods and dried guava for flavoring; sweet dried apples were too expensive. Soon after he returned, Ong Noi became very sick and died. After the family buried the grandfather, they left the village for safety from the fighting that was closing in on them. Some soldiers brought them to a fishing boat that carried them to a waiting ship. The young girl promised herself that she would someday return and bring her grandfather some sweet dried apples.

Key Understandings

The flora of an environment not only may provide beauty but also may be used for practical purposes. The people of Vietnam became very resourceful as a result of years of conflict and deprivation.

Knowledge

- Identify the relative location of Vietnam.
- Describe the flora of Vietnam.
- Explain the use of shelters during times of war.
- Compare the types of herbs used in Vietnam with those used in the United States.

Skills

- Ask questions about the location and flora of Vietnam.
- Ask questions about the shelters that Duc and his sister used.
- Gather information from library and primary sources.
- Organize information into a historical map representing the time frame of *Sweet Dried Apples*.
- Organize and categorize herbs into those that are medicinal, those used in cooking, and those used for aroma.
- Create a comparison chart of herbs used for a variety of purposes.
- Use a map of Vietnam to interpret the relationship between North and South Vietnam.
- Present information in a historical map, with an herb garden, and by designing a shelter.

Perspectives

Value the interaction between humans and the earth for the benefit of both.

Activities

I = Individual   P = Pairs   G = Group

A. ONG NOI'S WORLD (I)

Materials: globe, atlas, political map of Vietnam during the late 1960s, outline map of Vietnam, colored pencils, thin markers

Using the globe, find Southeast Asia and focus on Vietnam, noting the adjacent countries and bodies of water. Referring to the political map, draw the separation line between North and South Vietnam on the outline map. Identify the two capitals and other major cities in both countries. Color blue and label the bodies of water, including rivers. Find present-day Vietnam in the atlas and compare boundaries and city names.

Questions to Ask

1. What countries border Vietnam? What bodies of water?
2. What river delta is located in Vietnam? Why do you think it was important during the war and is still important today?
3. Where was Vietnam divided on the historical map?
4. How is Vietnam different today?
5. In comparing the modern map and the historical map of Vietnam, can you determine any results of the war in Ong Noi's world?

B. THE SECRET PLACE (I)

Materials: watercolor paper, watercolors, pencils, mat frame, masking tape

Have students interview either native Vietnamese people or soldiers who fought there about the shelters and tunnels that provided a safe haven for people during the war. The teacher should talk to the children about different types of peaceful places and how those compare to the shelters in Vietnam. Ask the children to draw and paint a picture of their secret place, real or imagined. Place a mat frame on the picture and tape it from the back. The teacher should make it clear that just as Duc and his sister were

Keeping the herb journal.

scolded by Ong Noi for not revealing their secret place, for safety reasons students should inform a parent about where their place is located. Students will present their watercolor paintings, describing and comparing their places to Duc and his sister's place. Describe how the uses for students' secret places are different from the uses for shelters during the war.

C. HERB GARDEN (G)

Materials: potting soil, clay pots, plastic potting tray, pebbles, watering can, trowel, plastic gloves, Popsicle-type sticks, white glue, 3 x 5-inch cards, ballpoint pens, herb seeds, small spiral notebook for plant journal

Each group of four or five students should investigate and select the types of herbs they would like to grow. Direct the students toward choosing herbs that are commonly used in cooking or for potpourri. The individuals in each group will each be responsible for potting, marking, and caring for one type of herb selected. Place herbs in the plastic tray in sunlight and watch them grow. Use a journal to keep a growth record and data on each herb. Once the plants have begun growing, groups should prepare a presentation about the herb garden, describing the uses for each individual herb.

Figure 10.1–Listening to My Environment
Hush!

HUMAN	ANIMAL
MECHANICAL	OTHER

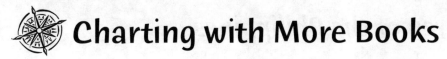 Charting with More Books

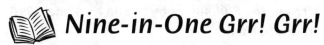 Nine-in-One Grr! Grr!

Projection: *Nine-in-One Grr! Grr!* told by Blia Xiong and adapted by Cathy Spagnoli, 1989
Genre: Folktale
Level: Primary (K–2)
Elements: II. Places and Regions; III. Physical Systems
Themes: Place; Region; Human/Environment Interaction

The Book

This Laotian tale tells of a time long ago when the first tiger, who wanted cubs, went to see the great sky god, Shao, to find out how many cubs she would have. Shao told her that she would have nine cubs a year only if she would remember his exact words. Because she had a bad memory, the tiger made a song to help her remember Shao's words. Happily, she walked the land singing, "Nine-in-one Grr! Grr!" over and over again. When the eu bird discovered the reason for the song, the bird knew that the tigers would soon devour all other animals. The bird tricked the tiger into singing the words "One-in-nine" instead. Thus it came to pass that there are not many tigers roaming the land.

The Lotus Seed

Projection: *The Lotus Seed* by Sherry Garland, 1997
Genre: Picture Storybook
Level: Bridge (2–4)
Elements: I. The World in Spatial Terms; II. Places and Regions; IV. Human Systems
Themes: Place; Region; Movement; Human/Environment Interaction

The Book

When the last emperor of Vietnam had to abdicate his throne, he was so overcome that he cried. The young girl who saw this went to the Imperial Garden and took a lotus seed. Since the lotus was the flower of her country, she would always keep the seed in remembrance of the young emperor. Wrapped in silk, the seed remained with her for good luck even when she became a wife and mother. When the war forced her to flee, she took her children and the seed to her new country.

One day her young grandson took the seed and planted it in the mud. Bà was sad until she saw how the seed blossomed into the beautiful lotus flower. She gave the seed from the pod to her granddaughter, who will relate to her children someday how Bà saw the emperor cry.

Children of the Philippines

Projection:	*Children of the Philippines* by Sheila Kinkade, 1996
Genre:	**Information Book**
Level:	**Bridge; Intermediate (2–6)**
Elements:	**I. The World in Spatial Terms; II. Places and Regions; III. Physical Systems; IV. Human Systems; V. Environment and Society**
Themes:	**Location; Place; Region; Human/Environment Interaction**

The Book

The reader is provided with a brief view of the lives of over a dozen Filipino children. The city environment as well as the countryside on the various Philippine islands, including the base of an active volcano, are shown. Children are pictured at school, working with their families, and playing games. Filipino traditions are passed on to the children. The boys of the Ifugao tribe, for example, are depicted gleefully performing the storylike Ifugao dance in traditional costumes. Girls of the Yakan tribal group learn very early in life how to weave cloth using unique traditional patterns. A concise introductory history of the islands is also presented.

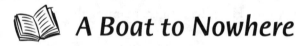 *A Boat to Nowhere*

Projection:	*A Boat to Nowhere* by Maureen Crane Wartski, 1980
Genre:	**Fiction; Chapter Book**
Level:	**Intermediate (4–6)**
Elements:	**I. The World in Spatial Terms; II. Places and Regions; IV. Human Systems**
Themes:	**Location; Place; Region; Movement; Human/Environment Interaction**

The Book

This exciting yet tragic story takes place in war-torn Vietnam. Mai and her family heard of impending doom and found themselves in the middle of the war. An orphan, Kien, joined the family on the *Sea Breeze* and sailed the South China Sea in search of freedom. Traveling on a very long journey through many hazards and after losing their grandfather, they finally found the key to the freedom they desperately sought. An American promised that their ordeal was over.

The Silent Lotus

Projection:	*The Silent Lotus* by Jeanne M. Lee, 1991
Genre:	Picture Storybook
Level:	Primary; Bridge (K–4)
Elements:	II. Places and Regions; IV. Human Systems
Themes:	Location; Place; Region

The Book

Beautiful watercolors adorn this touching story about a young mute girl, Lotus, living in ancient Kampuchea. Her parents took her to the temple to pray for a solution to her muteness. While there, she felt the vibrations of the drums and imitated the motions of the dancers. The king and queen were so impressed that they provided a dance teacher and assured Lotus's parents that she would learn to dance. Imitating the herons, cranes, and white egrets, she became a renowned dancer and performed in temples and palaces.

Realm References

Breckler, R. 1996. *Sweet Dried Apples: A Vietnamese Wartime Childhood.* Boston, MA: Houghton Mifflin Children's Books.

Cha, D. 1996. *Dia's Story Cloth.* New York: Lee and Low Books.

Garland, S. 1997. *The Lotus Seed.* San Diego, CA: Harcourt Brace.

Ho, M. 1996. *Hush! A Thai Lullaby.* New York: Orchard Books.

Kinkade, S. 1996. *Children of the Philippines.* Minneapolis, MN: Carolrhoda Books.

Lee, J. M. 1991. *The Silent Lotus.* New York: Farrar, Straus and Giroux.

Wartski, M. C. 1980. *A Boat to Nowhere.* New York: Penguin Books.

Xiong, B., adapted by C. Spagnoli. 1989. *Nine-in-One Grr! Grr!* San Francisco, CA: Children's Book Press.

Chapter 11
Australian Realm

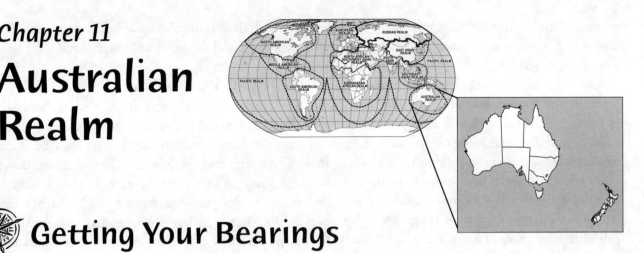

Getting Your Bearings

Location

This realm consists of an island continent, an island country, and a number of other islands located in the Southern Hemisphere. Australia and New Zealand, lying between the Indian and Pacific Oceans, are the focal points of the Australian Realm. Australia is arranged into six states and two territories: Western Australia, Queensland, South Australia, New South Wales, Victoria, Tasmania, Northern Territory, and Australian Capital Territory. Canberra, the capital city, is located in Australian Capital Territory. Australia is situated between latitudes 10°S and 44°S and longitudes 112°E and 154°E. New Zealand, consisting of two major islands, North Island and South Island, and a number of other smaller islands, is situated over a thousand miles southeast of Australia and is bounded by latitudes 34°S and 47°S and longitudes 166°E and 179°E. The capital of New Zealand is Wellington on the North Island. The total area of Australia is 2,967,909 square miles, and New Zealand, including North and South Islands, covers just over 103,736 square miles.

Topography

Australia is generally made up of low tablelands, with the exception of the Eastern Uplands, which include a series of high ridges, high plains, and plateaus. Mount Kosciusko is the highest mountain at 7,310 feet. Most of the Outback (interior land) is rangeland and desert, with only a small percent forested. Notable in this area is the world's oldest rock forma-

tion, Ayers Rock. The arable lands are located along the east and southwest coasts. The Great Barrier Reef off the northeast coast is the largest coral reef in the world. Both major islands of New Zealand are mountainous, with several mountains rising higher than any land mass in Australia. The Southern Alps on the South Island are the most notable range, with several peaks reaching higher than 11,700 feet and Mount Cook at 12,349 feet. A narrow plains area is found on the west coast of South and North Islands, with much of the land used as grazing land.

Climate

The seasons are reversed from those of North America. With the exception of Tasmania and Mount Kosciusko, which have snow in the winter, generally Australia is warm year-round, although the summer (December through February) temperature often exceeds 100°F. Rainfall is unevenly distributed throughout the country, with the climate being generally arid to semiarid. Most of the Outback receives annual rainfall of around 17 inches, with less in the desert areas. Along the north and east coasts as well as in the extreme southwest and western Tasmania, rainfall is plentiful. New Zealand boasts a temperate climate throughout, neither excessively hot nor cold, with an alpine climate in the Southern Alps.

Flora and Fauna

This realm exhibits unique flora and fauna. Among the animals and birds found in Australia are the magpie, satin bowerbird, kookaburra, crocodile, dingo, and wombat; marsupials, including the kangaroo, bandicoots, and koala; the distinctive monotremes (egg-laying mammals), the duck-billed platypus and the echidna; and flightless birds such as the emu. The Great Barrier Reef abounds with a variety of sealife, including the nudibranch, urn-shaped ascidians, foot-long flathead, and lionfish. Plant life common to the Outback includes tall 8-foot poles, the yacca-yacca, and a yamlike plant, the worwora. The eucalyptus forest grows along the Adelaide River, southeast of Darwin in Northern Territory. Some beautiful Outback flowers are the snake gourd and bladderwort. Tropical plants grow in Australia's tropical coastal areas, and temperate plants abound throughout New Zealand.

Unique Features

For many centuries, Australia and New Zealand were isolated from the rest of the world, creating unusual cultures, language, flora, and fauna. The Aborigines of Australia and the Maori of New Zealand developed unique cultures that are reflected in the languages and customs and traditions still evident today. Both countries are sparsely populated, with Australia's population over 18,500,000 and New Zealand's around 3,500,000. Both nations are large exporters of beef and wool.

Mapping

Punga, the Goddess of Ugly

Projection:	*Punga, the Goddess of Ugly* by Deborah Nourse Lattimore, 1993
Genre:	Picture Storybook
Level:	Bridge; Intermediate (2–6)
Elements:	I. The World in Spatial Terms; II. Places and Regions; IV. Human Systems
Themes:	Place; Region; Movement; Human/Environment Interaction

The Book

With secrets hidden in the pictures, this beautifully illustrated tale of twin Maori girls earning their *moko*, chin tattoo, leads the reader through Maori traditions and the flora and fauna of Aotearoa (New Zealand). While frolicking, Maraweia made an ugly face and ignored the warnings of her sister. Too late—she was captured by the Goddess of Ugly. Kiri challenged the Goddess of Ugly to release her sister so she could perform the fierce and beautiful haka dance with her. Kiri and Maraweia, sticking out their tongues while moving in this traditional dance, felt beautiful and happy. The key to success was to look beautiful while executing this dance. Once this was done, the *moko* was earned and the Goddess of Ugly was banished.

Key Understandings

Each culture creates unique features in response to its environment. These features are passed on through oral tradition, literature, and the arts.

Knowledge

- Identify the realm and region, noting flora and fauna.
- Describe the unique behavioral patterns of the two Maori girls that were passed on to them from their grandmother.
- Compare the *haka* to American folk dance (e.g., square dance and others).
- Contrast the traditional cultural features used by the Maori and the Hawaiians such as abodes, clothing, and tattoos.

- Indicate the changes in the Maori culture from the time of Kiri and Maraweia to the present.

Skills

- Develop a list of questions concerning past and present cultural features of the Maori.
- Gather information from multiple sources (e.g., library, Internet) about the Maori culture.
- Organize information into two categories, past and present, based on specific cultural features.
- Analyze the cultural information through the development of a comparison chart.
- Using the comparison chart, answer the questions posed in the beginning of the inquiry process.

Perspectives

Sensitivity to other cultures expands attitudes about diverse cultures.

Activities

I = Individual   P = Pairs   G = Group

A. PINPOINTING AOTEAROA (NEW ZEALAND) (G)

Materials: atlas, globe, graph paper with 1-inch squares, colored pencils, water markers, ruler

Create a geopolitical map of New Zealand, using appropriate colors and identifying with grid lines the location of North and South Islands. Color in and identify any surrounding bodies of water. Include a compass rose with cardinal and intermediate directions, legend, scale, principal meridians and parallels, and a title.

Questions to Ask

1. Between which parallels is New Zealand located? Between which meridians do you find New Zealand?
2. What is the relative location of the following: New Zealand to Australia? New Zealand to New Guinea? New Zealand to Antarctica?

Moko beauty triumphs over Punga.

3. In which hemisphere is New Zealand located? How does this location affect its seasons?
4. Using the scale of miles, what is the distance from the northernmost point to the southernmost point of the country?
5. What are some physical features of the islands? What are the country's major cities?
6. Where is the international dateline in relation to New Zealand? What is its purpose? Why do you think it is modified around New Zealand?

B. MAORI CULTURE (P)

Materials: atlas, globe, *National Geographic*, encyclopedia, information trade books

Compare Maori culture to your own culture. Research information that provides data about food, clothing, and traditions of past and modern Maori. Pay particular attention to music, dance, and body decorations. Record your information on a comparison chart. Repeat this procedure with your own culture. Determine the similarities between the Maori culture and your own. Are there any unique differences? Infer any relationships between the physical environment and the culture.

c. MAKING MOKO (I)

Materials: heavy paper plates, rulers, poster paints, scissors, masking tape, glue, colored construction paper, blue or black marking pens

On a paper plate, using poster paints, marking pen, construction paper, and any other interesting materials, create a face and mark a beautiful *moko* (tattoo) much like those formed on Kiri and her twin. Using masking tape, attach the ruler to the back of the decorated plate, forming a handle.

Repeat this procedure, making a mask for the Goddess of Ugly.

d. HAKA HIGH JINKS (P)

Materials: two masks (Goddess of Ugly and *moko*)

Choreograph a *haka* consisting of three parts. The first part should include various locomotions, such as leaping, running, and hopping. This part must be done with the tongue sticking out. In the second part, the dancer holds up the Goddess of Ugly (Punga) mask, and the motions should interpret the grotesque movements of Punga. During the final part of the dance, partners should hold up their *moko* masks, using motions that celebrate their victory over Punga.

Enoch the Emu

Projection:	*Enoch the Emu* by Gordon Winch, 1990
Genre:	Picture Storybook
Level:	Primary (K–2)
Elements:	I. The World in Spatial Terms; II. Places and Regions; III. Physical Systems
Themes:	Location; Place; Region

The Book

On a dusty plain in the far Australian Outback lived two flightless birds, emus, Enoch and his wife, Wilhelmina. Enoch fancied drinking billabong water with his mates at the Emu Club. His wife, who spent her time sitting in the nest warming nine olive-green eggs, was angry at him for not doing his share of parenting, so she took a vacation with her emu lady friends. Enoch had to keep his future family warm until hatching time. Should any dingos or foxes come near, he would frighten them away by making a loud booming noise with his throat.

Enoch took nesting very seriously, never leaving to eat or drink. He lost weight and his feathers became dull, yet he stayed. Eventually the nine olive-green eggs cracked and out stepped nine striped chicks. Enoch was so proud of being a father that he took his family to the Emu Club. His mates were so impressed that they wanted to do the same thing. They did, and continue to do the parenting today.

Key Understandings

The unique animal life of Australia developed in response to the characteristics of that location.

Knowledge

- Identify the location of Australia.
- Describe the land forms and climate of the Outback.

- Compare the various kinds of animals in the Outback to those found in the students' personal environment.

Skills

- Develop a list of questions concerning location and animal life of the Australian Outback.
- Gather information about the animal life of Australia and students' own environment (pictures, children's animal books, etc.).
- Organize the information into animals from the Outback and animals from the students' own environment.
- Determine how these animals are different and what role location plays in this difference.

Perspectives

Value the unique animals in different environments.

Activities

I = Individual   P = Pairs   G = Group

A. Finding Enoch's Place (G)

Materials: globe, student atlas with map, outline map of Australia, string, ruler, crayons, card stock, reproducible Australia Puzzle Map

Locate your home and Enoch's place on the globe, noting the location of the equator. Using the string, place one end at your home and stretch to the west until you reach Australia; do the same going east to Australia. Color in the continent of Australia on the outline map using beige or tan for the interior and green for the coastal areas. Identify the beige area as the Outback. Using the reproducible Australia Puzzle Map (see Figure 11.1 on page 134), arrange the puzzle pieces to form a map of Australia that matches the outline map.

Questions to Ask

1. The equator divides the globe into north and south. Is Enoch's place on the same side of the equator as your home? Is Enoch's place north of the equator or south of the equator?
2. In relation to other places on the globe (Canada, Africa, South America), is Australia near to or far from where you live?
3. Using your string as a reference, is Enoch's place closer going west or east?
4. Does Enoch live in the beige area or the green area on your outline map?
5. Based on the illustrations in the book, is Enoch's Outback like your home?

B. Mapping Australia's Animals (P, G)

Materials: colored outline map, children's magazines that focus on Australian animals, scissors, white glue, pencil

Search through the magazines for pictures of animals. Cut out and glue the animals to the colored outline map. Arrange in a pleasing manner in the Outback. Label the animals with names near each one. The teacher may do the labeling for those children who need additional help. Teacher and students should discuss the differences between the animals found in Australia and those in their own environment. Conclude the discussion with a connection between the location of Australia and the uniqueness of the animals found there.

C. Enoch's Make-believe Mates (I)

Materials: children's magazines with pictures, construction paper, colorful yarn, scissors, white glue, crayons, pencil

Find more pictures of Australian animals in the magazines. Cut out three different animals (e.g., kangaroo, emu, gecko), divide each one into three equal parts, and imagine ways to change their appearance by interchanging their heads, trunks, and legs. Put together your new animal by either cutting and pasting or drawing and coloring. Create a unique name for your animal. Fold construction paper in half to create a book. Title the front cover with the name of your new animal. Inside place Enoch's make-believe mate and write a story about it. Tie the book together with yarn and read your story to a friend.

Walkabout

Projection:	*Walkabout* by James V. Marshall, 1984
Genre:	Fiction; Chapter Book
Level:	Intermediate (4–6)
Elements:	I. The World in Spatial Terms; II. Places and Regions; III. Physical Systems; IV. Human Systems
Themes:	Location; Place; Region; Human/Environment Interaction

The Book

Two American children, a sister and brother named Mary and Peter, were victims of an air crash near the edge of the vast Sturt Desert in Australia. They began to walk to Adelaide, their destination, unaware that it was a thousand-mile trek. On their journey they met a bush boy, one of the native Aborigines who was undergoing the tribal rite of walkabout, the proving-of-manhood ritual in which he had to survive alone in the Outback for six months.

Because of her ignorance of the Aboriginal culture, Mary became fearful of the typical actions of the bush boy. The fear he saw in her eyes the boy misinterpreted as the *lubra*, the sign of his impending death. He knew he must lead them to safety, for without him they too would die.

The bush boy passed on his knowledge of the environment and survival skills to the children. These skills proved to be important because the bush boy caught a cold, developed a fever, and died. With confidence, the two completed their journey safely to the nearest settlement.

Key Understandings

Humans develop unique lifestyles, rituals, and artifacts that reflect the flora, fauna, land forms, and climate within an ecosystem.

Similarities in human characteristics cut across all cultures.

Knowledge

- Identify and describe the location of *Walkabout*.
- Design a map that displays information concerning this Outback location.

- Formulate mental maps concerning geographic features of the Outback.
- Contrast the geographic features of the Outback with other Australian regions.
- Identify the flora and fauna of *Walkabout* and describe how the Aborigines' lifestyles reflect this ecosystem.
- Compare and contrast the ecosystem reported in the book to that of students' own location.

Skills

- Generate questions related to the location and ecosystem of the Outback and the Aborigines found there.
- Locate and gather information concerning the Outback and Aborigines using library and Internet sources.
- Observe and record the human and physical charateristics of students' own location.
- Organize and analyze the data from the Outback and personal locations through maps and tables.
- Draw conclusions concerning similarities and differences in the bush boy's ecosystem and culture with students' own.

Perspectives

Understanding the patterns and processes of an ecosystem promotes appreciation of how humans adapt and respond to their environment.

Activities

I = Individual   P = Pairs   G = Group

A. Discovering the Bush Boy's Outback (G)

Materials: globe, intermediate atlas, colored pencils or crayons, markers, ruler, pencil

Find Australia on the globe. Note its isolation from the rest of the continents of the world. Using an intermediate atlas, draw an outline map of Australia. Develop a key that uses colors or patterns for various land forms (e.g., mountains, plateaus, hills, plains, deserts) and symbolic lines for state boundaries and rivers. Complete the map by coordinating colors and symbols with defined areas as identified in the atlas and key. Label each of the six Australian states with proper names, title the map, add a scale of miles, and include a compass rose.

Questions to Ask

1. Locating the Sturt Desert, how many miles do you estimate Mary and Peter walked from the plane crash site to safety at the settlement? How many miles was it from their crash site to their original destination, Adelaide?
2. What land forms can be found throughout the six Australian states?
3. What land forms, plants, and animals did the children observe during their trek through the Outback?
4. Why didn't Mary and Peter meet many people in the Outback? Why have so many people settled in the coastal areas?
5. How does the ecosystem of the Outback compare to your local ecosystem?

B. The Outback Eco-scene (P)

Materials: medium-size cardboard box (copy-paper cases work well), paint, brushes, glue, construction paper, and any other materials (e.g., sand, twigs, pebbles, etc.) required to produce a 3-D diorama

Investigate the Outback ecosystem for the flora and fauna found there. Collect pictures from books and magazines for reference purposes. To help reproduce them in the diorama, recall the plants and animals and land forms that Peter, Mary, and the bush boy observed on their walk. Remove the lid from the box. Place the box on its side and recreate the "Outback as the Outback Eco-scene" in the diorama.

C. Planning Your Personal Walkabout (I, G)

Materials: local map, compass, bus or train schedules, small spiral notebook for a journal, phone book

Utilizing the reference materials, plan a personal walkabout that encompasses a 5-mile radius around the school. In the journal, list eating places, interesting locales, modes of transportation, appropriate clothing, necessary resources (e.g., money, water), and essential safe places. Plot your walkabout, identifying points of interest, time limit, and stops along the way. Create a mental journey, record it in your journal, and share it with your group. Determine through group consensus whether this walkabout is workable.

Figure 11.1–Australia Puzzle Map
Enoch the Emu

1. DUPLICATE MAP PIECES ON CARD STOCK.
2. CUT OUT PIECES.
3. ARRANGE PIECES TO MATCH THE AUSTRALIAN CONTINENT.

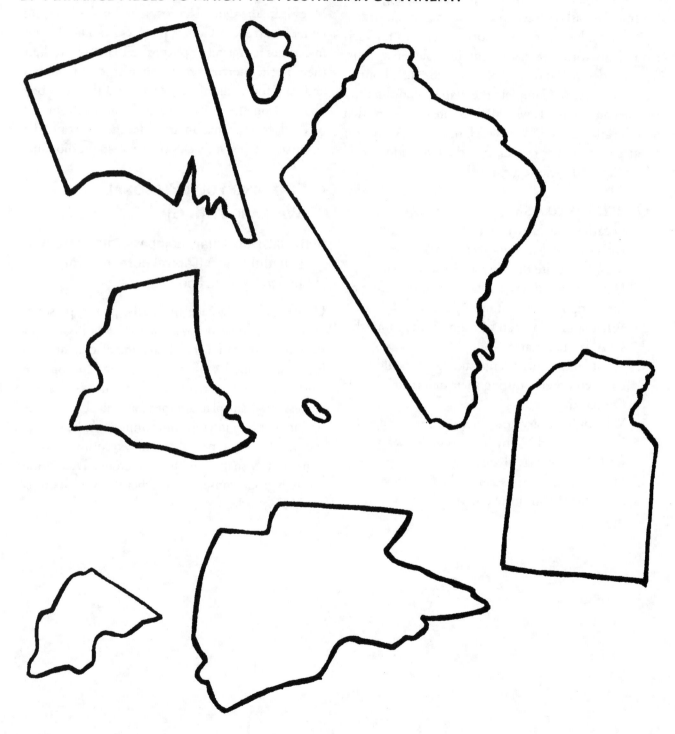

Charting with More Books

 ## *Farmer Schulz's Ducks*

Projection:	*Farmer Schulz's Ducks* by Colin Thiele, 1986
Genre:	Picture Storybook
Level:	Bridge; Intermediate (2–6)
Elements:	II. Places and Regions; IV. Human Systems; V. Environment and Society
Themes:	Location; Place; Human/Environment Interaction

The Book

The story takes place in Australia on a farm located near the Onkaparinga River. Farmer Schulz raised over fifty prized ducks and drakes of various types and colors. Each morning he would let the ducks out to cross the road so they could frolic in their natural habitat, the river. There were few cars, and the ducks crossed safely. As the year passed, the traffic became very heavy, and a drake was hit. None of the plans that the farmer and his family tried worked until the youngest child, Anna, came up with the idea to build a duck pipe under the road. The ducks and drakes now waddled safely through the pipe, over to their river, and back to the farm every day.

 ## *Snap!*

Projection:	*Snap!* by Marsha Vaughan, 1994
Genre:	Picture Storybook
Level:	Primary (K–2)
Elements:	I. The World in Spatial Terms; III. Physical Systems
Themes:	Location; Place

The Book

Joey, a baby kangaroo, decided to play games with his friends: Twisker, the bush mouse; Slider, the snake; Flatso, the platypus; and Prickler, the echidna. After playing hide-and-squeak, pass-the-mud-pie, and pick-up-quills, they came upon a crocodile, Sly Tooth, who played snap. Joey and his friends found themselves snapped right into the crocodile's jaws. They played tickle-the-tonsils, which caused Sly Tooth to open his jaws. Joey and his friends were saved.

John Midas in the Dreamtime

Projection: *John Midas in the Dreamtime* by Patrick Skene Catling, 1987
Genre: Fiction; Chapter Book
Level: Intermediate (4–6)
Elements: I. The World in Spatial Terms; II. Places and Regions; IV. Human Systems
Themes: Location; Place; Region

The Book

On a vacation to Australia, the Midas family traveled to the Outback to view the oldest rock formation on earth, Ayers Rock, located in Uluru National Park. The park ranger gave the family a history of the rock and described its original inhabitants and their story of creation, the Dreamtime. While his family was viewing the cave drawings, Young John strayed into one of the sacred caves forbidden to all but the Aborigines.

The cave narrowed into a small tunnel with several sharp turns that led to a bright desert landscape. Much to his surprise, John entered the Dreamtime.

Befriended by the Aborigines, he discovered that in this culture fire had not yet been discovered. They were eating raw meat and insects. To the amazement of the tribe, John demonstrated how to spark fire by moving a pointed stick vigorously in a log. During his stay, John experienced many other facets of this different culture.

Longing for his family, John was led to the spot where he had entered the Dreamtime. Walking back through the tunnel and out the cave entrance, he rejoined his family who seemed unaware of his adventure through time.

 # Koala Lou

Projection: *Koala Lou* by Mem Fox, 1989
Genre: Picture Storybook
Level: Primary (K–2)
Elements: II. Places and Regions; III. Physical Systems
Themes: Location; Place; Region

The Book

Koala Lou was a young koala bear who was loved by her mother and all of the other animals of the bush. As the years went by, other koalas were born and Koala Lou's mother didn't tell her that she loved her even though she still did. Koala Lou decided that she must enter the Bush Olympics in order to gain the favor of her mother once again. She trained and participated but only came in second. After the Olympics, she hid until dark and then went home. Once home, her mother hugged her and told her that she loved her. Koala Lou was happy again.

Realm References

Catling, P. S. 1987. *John Midas in the Dreamtime.* New York: Bantam Books.

Fox, M. 1989. *Koala Lou.* San Diego: Harcourt Brace.

Lattimore, D. N. 1993. *Punga, the Goddess of Ugly.* San Diego: Harcourt Brace.

Marshall, J. V. 1984. *Walkabout.* Littletown, MA: Sundance.

Thiele, C. 1986. *Farmer Schulz's Ducks.* New York: Harper and Row.

Vaughan, M. 1994. *Snap!* New York: Scholastic.

Winch, G. 1990. *Enoch the Emu.* Cairns, Australia: Childset.

Chapter 12
Pacific Realm

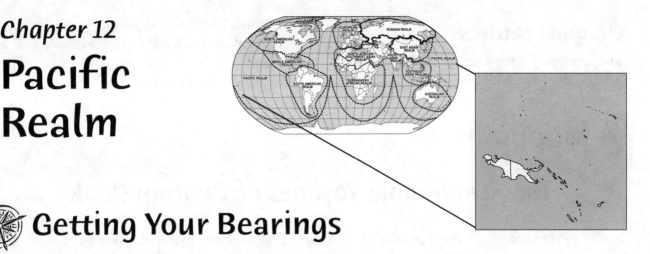

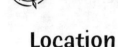 Getting Your Bearings

Location

This vast realm of 64,185,983 square miles, the largest of all the geographic realms, consists of tens of thousands of islands located in both the North and South Pacific. It consists of three regions: Melanesia, a group of islands just east of Indonesia, northeast of Australia, and extending beyond the Fiji Islands; Micronesia, north of Melanesia and east of the Philippines; and Polynesia, which stretches from the Hawaiian archipelago to Easter Island in the east and to just north of New Zealand. The Pacific Realm is situated between approximately 50°N and 30°S latitude and 130°E and 110°W longitude. Some of the major island groups in Melanesia include New Guinea, the Solomon Islands, the Fiji Islands, and New Caledonia. In Micronesia are many small islands, including the Marianas, the Marshall Islands, and Guam. Most notable in the Polynesian region are the Hawaiian Islands, Midway, Samoa, and French Polynesia.

Topography

The islands vary in their composition and include such forms as volcanic islands, coral atolls, and phosphate rocks. The volcanic islands, such as the Hawaiian and Tahitian groups, are mountainous in nature. The big island of Hawaii is the youngest of the Hawaiian chain, with active volcanic eruptions and continuous shoreline growth. This island has the world's highest mountain, when measured from its base on the ocean floor to its peak, Mauna Kea, nearly 32,000 feet high. French Polynesia is a mixture of rugged high islands and low islands with reefs.

Climate

The climate is primarily tropical and subtropical throughout the Pacific, with some variations based on mountain elevations. Snow may appear in the winter months on the peaks of the large shield volcanoes of Mauna Loa and Mauna Kea on the island of Hawaii and of Haleakala on Maui. The rainfall varies throughout the realm; in the Hawaiian Islands, for example, one side of an island may have over 100 inches of rainfall per year while the other side will have desert conditions. The island of Kauai is the wettest spot on earth, with an average of 460 inches of rainfall per year. The flatter coral atolls often have persistent problems with drought.

Flora and Fauna

Throughout the islands of the regions are found both luxuriant tropical and sparse desert vegetation, including hardwoods of the tropical rain forest, such as teak and mahogany. Some typical plants grown for export are coffee, tea, cocoa, bananas, pineapples, macadamia nuts, and coconuts. Other crops include cassava, taro, breadfruit, guava, papaw, and flowers such as orchids and hibiscus. A few of the animals in the realm are wild boar, mongoose, and the brilliant red bird i'iwi. Hawaiian National Wildlife Refuges are home to millions of seabirds, including the greater frigate bird, booby, and albatross. In the ocean are found monk seals, whales, and, in Hawaii, the green turtle as well as typical coral-reef sealife.

Unique Features

The population of the islands of the Pacific is around 10,293,000. The cultures are ethnically diverse, with Polynesian, Chinese, and Japanese peoples being most prevalent. The travel and tourism industry has capitalized on the tropical climate throughout the realm as a destination for sun worshipers.

 # Mapping

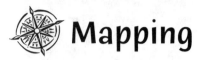 ## *The Remarkable Voyages of Captain Cook*

Projection:	*The Remarkable Voyages of Captain Cook* by Rhoda Blumberg, 1991
Genre:	Nonfiction; Chapter Book
Level:	Intermediate (4–6)
Elements:	I. The World in Spatial Terms; II. Places and Regions; III. Physical Systems
Themes:	Location; Place; Region

The Book

The book follows Captain Cook's expeditions in the Pacific Ocean in search of the "unknown southern continent" and a Northwest Passage. The voyages are described with a special emphasis on physical and cultural geography and on the people and their languages, customs, dress, and abodes encountered during his journeys. The observations of the naturalist Joseph Banks and the drawings by artists who were on the voyages give an authentic and unique quality to the text.

Although Cook failed to discover the southern continent or the Northwest Passage, his accomplishments were quite extraordinary: He charted large areas of the Pacific; observed and reported on the culture of the peoples; advocated the collection of natural history data[1]; and proved that survival on long sea voyages was possible with a healthy diet and cleanliness aboard ship.

Key Understandings

The expeditions of Captain Cook improved navigational technology and the feasibility of long voyages. Investigating the flora and fauna of new lands increases knowledge and understanding of the cultures of people in diverse locations.

Knowledge

- Identify the realm, define the regions within it, and describe the land forms and flora and fauna found in each region.
- Depict the cultures of the people living within these regions.
- Distinguish the routes of Cook's three voyages, noting ports of call, impediments, and advantages.
- Discuss the ramifications of Cook's voyages.
- Compare and contrast Cook's navigational methods with modern technology.

Skills

- Map the three voyages from the point of debarkation in England to their conclusion.
- Plot latitude and longitude of the ports of call on Cook's voyages.

---

[1]The work of the eighteenth-century English naturalist Sir Joseph Banks, who was an integral part of Cook's explorations, is featured in *National Geographic*'s November 1996 issue. The descriptions and pictures of his collections are relevant for study of the Pacific Realm.

- Gather information about the physical and cultural geography found at these diverse locations.
- Using the maps as a framework, analyze the physical and cultural patterns.
- Present generalizations concerning the cultural patterns in a creative manner.

Perspectives

Acknowledge the contributions of Captain Cook to the advancement of world geography. Appreciate the varied cultures of the Pacific Realm.

THE FIRST VOYAGE—THE *ENDEAVOUR*

Captain Cook's Log: Left England August 1768. Navigated Cape Horn. Sailed to Tahiti, New Zealand, Australia, Java. Cape Horn back to England, July 12, 1771.

On this voyage Banks collected unique specimens at all the places visited. Cook and Banks also reported their observations about the peoples they met as well as their uncommon customs: Tahitian men blew on flutes through their noses; the young girls were tattooed over specific parts of their bodies (Banks started a naval tradition by also being tattooed); and the cannibalistic Maori of New Zealand ate their enemies to absorb their courage and strength.

Activities

I = Individual   P = Pairs   G = Group

A. SAILING COOK'S REALM (G)

Materials: globe, Mercator projection map of the world, yarn, pushpins, map of the first voyage

Using the first voyage map as a guide, plot Cook's route by placing pushpins at the appropriate locations in the large Mercator projection attached to a wall. String the yarn between the pushpins so that the route will be clearly represented. Students investigate the flora and fauna of each of the places visited. Either draw or cut out a small picture that represents one example of something that was found at each port of call and place them appropriately on the large wall map.

Questions to Ask

1. Through which oceans did the *Endeavour* pass?
2. What continents did Cook pass? Which ones did he visit?
3. What islands did Cook pass? Which ones did he visit?
4. If you were the captain of the *Endeavour*, what provisions would you take on board for this long voyage? Give your reasons for your choices. How do Cook's choices compare to yours?
5. What provisions could you get at the islands and continents that Cook visited? How would these supplement his provisions?
6. Acting in the role of Banks, the naturalist, what significant flora and fauna would you choose to take back to England?

B. CULTURE CHARADES (P)

Choose a port of call and investigate the curious customs of the peoples of that land. Determine and perform the movements necessary to project two or more customs that would represent those peoples in a game of charades.

THE SECOND VOYAGE—THE *RESOLUTION* AND THE *ADVENTURE*

Captain Cook's Log: Left England July 1772. Navigated Cape of Good Hope. Sailed through the Antarctic Circle. Continued on to New Zealand, Tahiti, and the Tonga Islands. Crossed the Antarctic Circle twice. Sailed to Easter Island, the Marquesas Islands, and once again to Tahiti. Entered Melanesia, visited New Hebrides [now Vanuatu], and discovered New Caledonia. Ventured across the Antarctic Circle again. Passed Cape Horn to South Georgia, the Sandwich Islands [now Hawaii], and back to England, 1780.

Frustrated by not discovering the southern continent, Cook requested permission from the Admiralty to lead a second and longer voyage that was to be the first Antarctic expedition. To help overcome the persistent problem of determining longitude, for this trip Cook installed chronometers, timepieces set

Planning the trip.

to Greenwich, England, time that could withstand the ship's rolling and varied temperatures. By comparing local ship time (observation of sun and stars) with chronometer time, Cook became the first navigator to know his approximate location.

Although he failed to reach Antarctica in his two attempts, Cook did conclude that there could be a large tract of land near the South Pole that was the undiscovered continent.

Activities

I = Individual   P = Pairs   G = Group

A. Sailing the Second Voyage (I, P)

Materials: globe, Mercator projection of the world, 8.5 x 11-inch reproduction of a Mercator projection with grid lines for each student, pencils, marking pens, distance worksheet

On the student Mercator projection reproduction, locate and trace with marking pen and label 0° grid lines for zero latitude and longitude. On the grid lines, mark degrees of latitude and longitude, including the Antarctic Circle. Note the cardinal directions on the map as defined by the zero degrees of latitude and longitude (north above 0° latitude, south below 0° latitude, east and west to either side of 0° longitude). Using the log and the map of the second voyage, make a list of important ports of call and determine both the absolute and relative locations.

Questions to Ask

1. In which direction did Cook go when initially leaving England?
2. Through which hemispheres did Cook pass?
3. What is the absolute location of the Cape of Good Hope, using latitude and longitude? New Zealand? Tahiti? Easter Island? New Hebrides? New Caledonia? Cape Horn?
4. What is the relative location of the following: New Zealand to the Antarctic Circle? Cape of Good Hope to the Antarctic Circle? Tahiti to Easter Island? New Caledonia to England? Cape Horn to the Antarctic Circle?
5. How many degrees of latitude are there between England and the Antarctic Circle? How many degrees of longitude are there between England and New Caledonia?
6. Using the information about the hemispheres through which Cook passed and the absolute and relative location of the places Cook visited, formulate a conclusion about his accomplishments as a navigator.

B. Vacation Log (I)

Materials: spiral notebook, magazines, travel brochures, scissors, pens, pencils, glue, personal-size Mercator projection of the world, globe, air map

Students should view the Pacific Realm on the globe and select three islands that they would like to visit. Research the chosen islands to determine location, physical geography, flora and fauna, climate, and culture of the islanders. Using the air map (map of air routes), determine the path that your airplane would follow from the beginning to the end of the journey. Plot this itinerary on the Mercator projection. Identify the clothing, medicine, and equipment necessary to ensure an enjoyable vacation. For each port of call, record adventures, including a description of the landscape, peoples, interesting sites, and activities. In the student vacation log, record information related to this vacation, including maps, itinerary, plans, postcards, pictures, and experiences. Share the vacation log with parent(s) and other students.

THE THIRD VOYAGE—THE *RESOLUTION* AND THE *DISCOVERY*

Captain Cook's Log: Left England 1776. Navigated Cape Horn to Tahiti, going north. Discovered Kauai, Hawaii. Continued on to the west coast of North America and Vancouver Island searching for the Northwest Passage. Moved along the Alaskan peninsula, the Aleutian Islands, and the Bering Strait. Headed south back to Hawaii. Unfinished log. [Cook was murdered February 14, 1779.] Ships under new captains followed Cook's itinerary and returned to England.

The object of the third voyage was to discover a passage through or above Canada connecting the Atlantic and Pacific Oceans and providing a trade route to China. After stops in New Zealand and Tahiti, Cook headed north and discovered Kauai. He reported that the natives resembled and spoke somewhat like the Tahitians, who resided 3,000 miles away. Traveling north along the Alaskan peninsula, he passed the Aleutian Islands and went on to the Bering Strait, where he traced in detail the Asian and Alaskan shores. After his return to one of the Hawaiian islands, Hawaii, a theft caused Cook to attempt to use the Hawaiian king as hostage. The natives, however, foiled his plan and killed Cook in the process.

Activities

I = Individual   P = Pairs   G = Group

A. THE HAWAIIAN ISLANDS: HAWAII, COOK'S LAST PORT OF CALL (P)

Materials: geopolitical map of the Hawaiian Islands, relief map, wax crayon, supplementary materials about Hawaii (atlas, related issues of *National Geographic*), watercolor paints, paintbrushes, heavy corrugated cardboard (preferably a box cover), geodough (salt, flour, water), black marking pen

Set the latitude and longitude grid using a wax crayon on the inside of the box lid. Draw the outline of the islands on this grid. Using the maps as a guide, fill in the outline of each island with the geodough. Place a sufficient amount on each island so as to mold mountain areas, giving each island a three-dimensional shape. Check elevations of the land forms on each island. Shape the land according to elevation and form (beach, mountain, mountain range, plain, plateau). Paint each level in the following colors: 0 (sea level) to 2,000 feet, green; 2,000 to 4,000 feet, yellow; 4,000 to 6,000 feet, brown. Paint the water light blue, making sure to cover the entire box lid. Identify each island in an adjacent spot in the water with black marking pen. In the upper right-hand corner, title the map. Establish a scale of miles and an elevation key beneath the title.

Questions to Ask

1. Between what lines of longitude are the Hawaiian Islands? Latitude?
2. What is the relative location of Kauai to Hawaii? Kauai to Maui? Would it be easy or difficult for Cook to travel between these islands? Why?
3. Which island has the highest elevation? Which has the lowest?
4. Which island has the most volcanoes? Which has the highest volcano? Which island has active volcanoes? What is the difference between a Hawaiian shield volcano and a composite-cone volcano?
5. On which island did Cook die? What is the name of the place where Cook was murdered? What is its approximate location?

B. STATE OF HAWAII'S DATA (G)

Materials: Internet, CD-ROM, encyclopedia, geography books, brochures, maps, reproducible charts and map

Students should investigate from a variety of sources, in and outside the classroom, information relating to the population and ethnic groups of the State of Hawaii. Use reproducible (see Figure 12.1 on page

146) to present your data. Choose one of the islands and determine what industries (goods and services) are located there. Calculate the revenue gained from those goods and services. Compile the data for each island in graph form on reproducible (see Figure 12.2 on page 147). Answer the questions listed below each graph. On the reproducible map (see Figure 12.3 on page 148), label the islands and develop a key for each of the goods and services. Draw the appropriate symbols for the island. Share and gather information from other students about other islands and complete the map. What conclusions can be drawn for the islands from the graphed data?

c. HAWAIIAN ROCK HOUNDS (I, P)

Materials: books about rocks, magazine pictures, brochures, drawing materials, poster board, sample rocks

Using the Internet and library sources, research information about shield volcanoes to determine the following: shape, composition of eruptions, and rock formations. Identifying the volcanic rocks formed after the lava cooled, compile a rock profile that includes pictures, drawings, or rocks (if available) with descriptions. Collect rock samples from the local area. Compare these to the Hawaiian volcanic rocks. Present this information as an exhibit for other students.

The Toad that Taught Flying

Projection:	*The Toad that Taught Flying* by Malia Maness, 1993
Genre:	Picture Storybook
Level:	Primary (K–2)
Elements:	I. The World in Spatial Terms; III. Physical Systems
Themes:	Location; Place

The Book

In his first try at flying, Kama, a baby mynah bird, fell through a ginger plant and landed with a thud on the ground. The gecko laughed at his failure. A toad showed the sad Kama how to hop like he did. Although in his first few attempts Kama was very clumsy, the toad encouraged the bird to try flapping his wings a little with each hop. Kama found that the more he hopped and the harder he flapped, the higher he flew. Soon he was flying. As he flew higher and higher, objects below became smaller and smaller. He now had his own bird's-eye view of the house with the tin roof, the truck, the trees, and the tiny toad. Kama thanked the toad, his friend and flying instructor, for helping him believe that, with practice, he could fly.

Key Understandings

A map is a projection of a location and place based on a bird's-eye view. Different locations have unique fauna.

Knowledge

- Locate the Hawaiian Islands on a globe.
- Demonstrate the concept of mapping (bird's-eye view) through movement and illustration.
- Describe the fauna of the location as depicted in the story.
- Compare and contrast the fauna from the story to that of students' own location.

Skills

- Develop questions concerning what can be seen from Kama's bird's-eye view, with emphasis on the fauna.

- Gather information about bird's-eye views from different sources: story illustration, table map, and primary atlas.
- Organize and analyze information based on the relative distance above location.
- Answer questions about Kama's bird's-eye view.

Perspectives

Value the fauna of different locations. Appreciate bird's-eye view.

Activities

I = Individual   P = Pairs   G = Group

A. FLYING OVER KAMA'S WORLD (P, G)

Materials: globe, primary atlas, miniature objects, table map, drawing paper, crayons, pencils, copies of illustrations from the story

Using the globe, find Kama's home, the Hawaiian Islands, noting their location in the Pacific Ocean. Discover on the globe the location of the students' home, comparing similarities and contrasting differences. Using table map with miniature objects, primary atlas, and illustrations from the story, compare and contrast the various perspectives of bird's-eye view.

Questions to Ask

1. What is the location of Kama's world and the students' world?
2. What physical features are seen at each location? How are they similar? How are they different?
3. From Kama's flying view, what objects can be seen in the story illustration? How would these objects look as seen by the toad and the gecko on the ground?
4. From your flying view of the table map, what objects can be seen? How would these objects look from a ground view?
5. Looking at the illustration, the table map, and the atlas map, what similarities and differences can you find?

6. In what ways are mapping and bird's-eye view the same?

B. LOCOMOTION THEATER (G)

Materials: copies of the story, table map, colored highlighters

The class should be divided into two groups: readers and movers. Each reader will be provided with a copy of the story with individual parts highlighted. As the readers narrate their parts, the movers interpret the text with appropriate movement. While maneuvering around the room, the movers should be directed to observe the miniature objects on the table map. Next, have the readers and movers exchange places and repeat the activity.

C. LOCOMOTION MAP (I)

Materials: drawing paper, crayons, pencil

Pretending to be Kama flying over the classroom, have students make a mental map of the objects seen. Based on their observations during "Locomotion Theater," students will draw and color a map of the classroom using the materials provided. The completed locomotion maps should be posted around the room. A class discussion about the differences in perspective should follow.

D. LOCO-FAUNA CHART (P)

Materials: poster board, glue, magazines with fauna pictures from Hawaii and student locale, scissors

Divide the class into two groups: Hawaiian fauna and local fauna. Each group will find and cut out pictures of fauna from materials provided. They will categorize the fauna according to "airborne" and "grounded" types. Using the poster board, students will make charts by gluing appropriate pictures under each heading. Display the charts and conduct a discussion comparing fauna from both locations.

Figure 12.1–Ethno-Graphing Hawaii

Ethnic Population Hawaii

(thousands)

	Polynesian	Japanese	Chinese	European	Other
100					
90					
80					
70					
60					
50					
40					
30					
20					
10					

DIRECTIONS: RESEARCH THE ETHNIC INFORMATION FOR THE HAWAIIAN ISLANDS.

1. COLOR IN THE BOXES ON THE CHART PROVIDED.
2. ANSWER THESE QUESTIONS:
    A. WHAT ARE THE LARGEST AND SECOND-LARGEST ETHNIC GROUPS IN THE STATE?

    B. WHAT IS THE SMALLEST ETHNIC GROUP?

    C. WHAT REASONS MIGHT THERE BE FOR THE ETHNIC MAKE UP OF THE ISLANDS?

Figure 12.2–Industry-Graphing Hawaii

Industries (Goods and Services of _____)

(thousands)

	Tourism	Pineapple	Flowers	Sugar	Other
100					
90					
80					
70					
60					
50					
40					
30					
20					
10					

DIRECTIONS: RESEARCH THE INDUSTRIES (GOODS AND SERVICES) OF THE SELECTED ISLAND. DISCOVER THE YEARLY REVENUE FOR EACH INDUSTRY LISTED ON THE CHART.

1. LABEL EACH COLUMN ACCORDING TO THE FOUR MAJOR INDUSTRIES FOUND THERE.
2. COLOR IN THE BOXES ON THE CHART PROVIDED.
3. ANSWER THESE QUESTIONS:
    A. WHAT IS THE MOST IMPORTANT INDUSTRY FOR YOUR ISLAND?

    B. WHAT REASONS CAN YOU GIVE FOR THIS?

Figure 12.3—Island Goods and Services Mapping

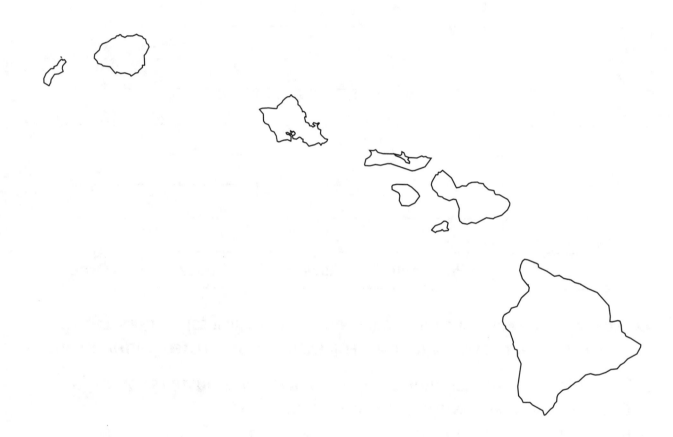

DIRECTIONS: USE AN ATLAS AND YOUR DATA FROM "INDUSTRY-GRAPHING HAWAII" TO COMPLETE THE MAP.

1. LABEL THE ISLANDS.
2. CREATE A KEY WITH SYMBOLS FOR GOODS AND SERVICES.
3. DRAW THE SYMBOLS FOR YOUR ISLAND ON THE MAP.
4. GATHER INFORMATION FROM CLASSMATES ABOUT THE OTHER ISLANDS AND COMPLETE THE MAP.

Charting with More Books

 ## *Tutu and the Ti Plant*

Projection: *Tutu and the Ti Plant* by Sandra L. Goforth, 1993
Genre: Picture Storybook
Level: Bridge (2–4)
Element: I. The World in Spatial Terms; IV. Human Systems;
V. Environment and Society
Themes: Location; Place

The Book

A Hawaiian grandmother, a tutu (one who designs quilts that tell of native plants), shared the stories of the Ti plant with her children. The woody plant within the lily family was used by ancient and modern natives for wrapping foods for baking, for fishing, and for thatching roofs. Most of all, the Ti plant was considered to bring good luck. Directions for making the Ti quilt, a lei, and a laulau are included.

Pearl Harbor Is Burning! A Story of World War II

Projection: *Pearl Harbor Is Burning! A Story of World War II* by Kathleen V. Kudlinski, 1993
Genre: Fiction
Level: Bridge; Intermediate (2–6)
Element: I. The World in Spatial Terms; II. Places and Regions
Themes: Location; Place; Movement

The Book

Set on the Hawaiian island of Oahu in December 1941, the plot centers on Frank, a young boy, new from the mainland, and Kenji, a Japanese-American islander. While playing in a treehouse, the two had a bird's-eye view of the Japanese attack on Pearl Harbor. Through Kenji, Frank learned of the traditions of a new culture, which strengthened their friendship despite the realities of war.

Warriors, Wigmen, and the Crocodile People: Journeys in Papua New Guinea

Projection:	*Warriors, Wigmen, and the Crocodile People: Journeys in Papua New Guinea* by Barbara A. Margolies, 1993
Genre:	**Information Book**
Level:	**Intermediate (4–6)**
Elements:	**I. The World in Spatial Terms; II. Places and Regions; III. Physical Systems; IV. Human Systems; V. Environment and Society**
Themes:	**Location; Place; Region; Movement; Human/Environment Interaction**

The Book

The book provides a view of life in two different cultures in Papua New Guinea. The tribal groups in these communities carry on traditional rites and customs. The Sepic River people, who live in stilt houses, are known for their ceremonial song and dance festivals as well as their ritual scarring. In the Huli Wig village, the men paint their faces in unique patterns and wear colorful headdresses of feathers and flowers. The accompanying colorful photographs enhance the text.

From Sea to Shining Sea, Hawaii

Projection:	*From Sea to Shining Sea, Hawaii* by Dennis B. Fradin, 1994
Genre:	**Information Book**
Level:	**Bridge Intermediate (2–6)**
Elements:	**I. The World in Spatial Terms; II. Places and Regions; III. Physical Systems; IV. Human Systems**
Themes:	**Location; Place; Region**

The Book

This colorful, picture-filled book about the State of Hawaii provides information on the history, peoples, and products of the land called "Paradise." The cultural geography and physical geography of eight of the islands in the Hawaiian chain are described.

Realm References

Blumberg, R. 1991. *The Remarkable Voyages of Captain Cook.* New York: Bradbury Press.

Fradin, D. B. 1994. *From Sea to Shining Sea, Hawaii.* Chicago: Children's Press.

Goforth, S. L. 1993. *Tutu and the Ti Plant.* Honolulu: MnM Publishing.

Kudlinski, K. V. 1993. *Pearl Harbor Is Burning! A Story of World War II.* New York: Puffin Books.

Maness, M. 1993. *The Toad that Taught Flying.* Camuela, HI: Pacific Greetings.

Margolies, B. A. 1993. *Warriors, Wigmen, and the Crocodile People: Journeys in Papua New Guinea.* New York: Four Winds Press.

Watkins, T. H. 1996. "The Greening of the Empire, Sir Joseph Banks." *National Geographic* 190(5):28–53.

Glossary

Absolute location: Position of a certain place on the surface of the earth or on a map, stated in degrees, minutes, and seconds of latitude and longitude.

Area: Any specific geographic entity.

Arid: Areas that are parched and lack moisture.

Ash-cinder volcano: Volcanic cone formed by layers of ash and cinders.

Climate: The prevailing temperature and meteorological weather conditions over a period of time.

Continent: One of the major land masses of the earth.

Cultural geography: The study of the relationship between humans and their environment.

Culture: The language, traditions, arts, religion, institutions, and shared history of people in a specific period of time.

Delta: A triangular, low-lying area of alluvial deposits formed around a river mouth.

Desert: Barren, arid area noted for its low rainfall and extremes of heat and cold.

Ecological perspective: Perception and inquiry of the connections and relationships among life forms, ecosystems, and human societies.

Ecosystem: A system of interacting and interdependent organisms in their natural environment.

Environment: The surrounding natural area.

Equator: An imaginary line drawn around the globe, equidistant from the North and the South Poles, setting the lines of latitude and dividing the Northern and Southern Hemispheres.

Fault line: The path along which the earth fractures during times of great stress.

Fauna: Animals of a realm or region.

Fiction: Prose literature that emphasizes the imaginary and fanciful.

Flora: Vegetation of a realm or region.

Geography: The study of the earth's physical and cultural features and phenomena.

Glacier: A mass of slow-moving snow and ice.

Global warming: Heating of the atmosphere as a result of burning fossil fuels and other factors ("greenhouse effect") that could melt the polar ice caps.

Globe: A spherical map of the world projected through a grid system of longitude and latitude lines.

Habitat: The natural environment where specific people, animals, and plants live.

Hemisphere: Half of the globe, divided north and south by the equator, divided east and west by the prime meridian.

International Date Line: The imaginary line of longitude following the 180th meridian that is the designated point where each new day begins.

Latitude: The distance of a place north or south of the equator, measured in degrees (0° to 90°) along parallel lines aligned east and west around the globe.

Lava volcano: A volcanic cone with a vent from which hot, flowing, molten matter is expelled.

Longitude: The distance of a place measured in degrees (0° to 180°) east or west from the prime meridian at Greenwich, England.

Magma: Hot molten rock underneath the earth's crust, created by the meltdown of the earth's crust and mantle.

Mental map: An individual's perception and recording of the spatial features of an area or place.

Meridian: A line of longitude drawn north-south on a globe and converging with other meridians at both poles.

Monsoon: A seasonal wind that results in the rainy season in South and Southeast Asia from April to October.

Nonfiction: Prose literature that focuses on reality and accurate information.

Oasis: A fertile green spot where there is water in a desert.

Outback: Australia's isolated inland areas.

Parallel: A line of latitude drawn east-west on a globe, measuring distance north or south of the equator.

Physical geography: The study of the physical features of a place.

Plateau: A large, flat-topped, elevated area of land.

Projection: A flat image of the earth's curved surface on a map.

Realm: A spatial framework of lands or countries that is based on common physical and/or cultural geographic landscapes.

Region: An area within a geographic realm that exhibits homogeneity based on selected criteria (e.g., land forms, language group, etc.)

Relative location: The position of a certain place on the surface of the earth using surrounding locations as reference points.

Savannah: A grassy plain located in tropical or subtropical areas such as Subsaharan Africa.

Scale of miles: A fixed, ordered series of units used in cartography to measure mileage.

Spatial perspective: Perception, inquiry, and appreciation of the dimensions of space and place and spatial patterns and processes.

Steppe: A vast plain with few or no trees located in Eurasia.

Taiga: An evergreen forest found in the northern regions of Eurasia and North America.

Tectonic plates: Pieces of the earth's crust that are constantly moving.

Topography: The physical configuration of a place, region, or realm.

Tsunami: A tidal wave created by seismic action.

Tundra: Treeless, frozen subsoil found in Arctic regions.

Bibliography

European Realm

Anno, M. 1985. *Anno's Britain.* New York: Philomel Books.

Bemelmans, L. 1993. *Madeline's Rescue.* New York: Viking Penguin.

Bradford, K. 1992. *There Will Be Wolves.* New York: Lodestar Books.

Brown, M. 1971. *Cinderella.* New York: Macmillan.

Carlson, N. S. 1986. *The Family Under the Bridge.* New York: Harper and Row Junior Books.

Cohen, B. 1987. *Even Higher.* New York: Lothrop, Lee and Shepard Books.

Connolly, P. 1989. *Tiberius Claudius Maximus: The Cavalry Man.* New York: Oxford University Press.

dePaola, T. 1975. *Strega Nona.* New York: Simon and Schuster.

———. 1993. *Strega Nona Meets Her Match.* New York: G. P. Putnam's Sons.

Doherty, B. 1990. *White Peak Farm.* New York: Orchard Books.

Eldridge, M. E. 1983. *In My Garden.* London: The Medici Society.

Fern, E. 1993. *Pepito's Story.* New York: Bantam Books.

Fix, P. 1994. *Not So Very Long Ago: Life in a Small Country Village.* New York: Dutton Children's Books.

Foreman, M. 1991. *War Boy.* London: Pavilion Books.

Goodall, J. 1987. *The Story of a Main Street.* New York: Macmillan.

Hardy, T. 1996. *Lost Cat.* Boston: Houghton Mifflin Children's Books.

Hutton, W. 1994. *Persephone.* New York: Macmillan.

Jacobs, F. 1994. *A Passion for Danger: Nansen's Arctic Adventures.* New York: Putnam.

Kelly, E. 1966. *The Trumpeter of Krakow.* New York: Macmillan Publishing.

Kismaric, C. 1988. *The Rumor of Pavel and Paali.* New York: Harper and Row.

Kunhardt, E. 1987. *Pompeii … Buried Alive!* New York: Random House.

Lamorisse, A. 1990. *The Red Balloon.* New York: Delacorte Press.

Lingard, J. 1992. *Tug of War.* New York: Puffin Books.

Lowry, L. 1989. *Number the Stars.* New York: Dell.

Marshak, S. 1989. *The Pup Grew Up!* New York: Henry Holt.

Mathers, P. 1995. *Kisses from Rosa.* New York: Alfred A. Knopf.

Matthews, W. 1995. *The Gift of a Traveler.* Mahwah, NJ: BridgeWater Books.

McCaffrey, A. 1996. *Black Horses for the King.* San Diego: Harcourt Brace.

McMillan, B. 1995. *Nights of the Pufflings.* Boston: Houghton Mifflin.

Morpurgo, M. 1983. *Twist of Gold.* New York: Viking.

Pausewang, G. P. Crampton, trans. 1996. *The Final Journey.* New York: Viking.

Provensen, A., and M. Provensen. 1987. *The Glorious Flight.* New York: Puffin Books.

Reiss, J. 1972. *The Upstairs Room.* New York: Harper and Row Junior Books.

Sis, P. 1996. *Starry Messenger.* New York: Farrar, Straus and Giroux.

Spyri, J. 1996. *Heidi.* New York: Viking Children's Books.

Szablya, H. M., and P. K. Anderson. 1996. *The Fall of the Red Star.* Honesdale, PA: Caroline House.
Wisniewski, D. 1996. *Golem.* New York: Clarion Books.

Russian Realm

Brewster, H. 1996. *Anastasia's Album.* New York: Hyperion Books for Children.
Croll, C. 1996. *The Little Snowgirl.* New York: The Putnam and Grosset Group.
Hesse, K. 1992. *Letters from Rifka.* New York: Henry Holt.
Kendall, R. 1994. *Russian Girl: Life in an Old Russian Town.* New York: Scholastic.
Lasky, K. 1986. *The Night Journey.* New York: Viking Kestrel.
McCurdy, M. 1987. *The Devils Who Learned to Be Good.* Boston: Joy Street Books.
Polacco, P. 1988. *Rechenka's Eggs.* New York: Philomel Books.
——. 1993. *Babushka Baba Yaga.* New York: Philomel Books.
Pushkin, A. Trans. and retold by P. T. Lowe. 1975. *The Tale of the Czar Saltan, or the Prince, and the Swan Princess.* New York: Thomas Y. Crowell.
Ransome, A. 1991. *The Fool of the World and the Flying Ship.* New York: A Sunburst Book/Farrar, Straus and Giroux.
Sherman, J. 1988. *Vassilisa the Wise: A Tale of Medieval Russia.* San Diego: Harcourt Brace Jovanovich.
Stanley, D. 1986. *Peter the Great.* New York: Four Winds Press.
Winthrop, E. 1997. *The Little Humpbacked Horse.* New York: Clarion Press.
Wolkstein, D. 1991. *Oom Razoom, or, Go I Know Not Where, Bring Back I Know Not What.* New York: Morrow Junior Books.

North American Realm

Appelt, K. 1995. *Bayou Lullaby.* New York: William Morrow.
Beattie, O., and J. Geiger. 1992. *Buried in Ice: The Mystery of a Lost Arctic Expedition.* New York: Scholastic.
Bowman, L. W. 1989. *The Canada Geese Quilt.* New York: Cobblehill Books.
Brandenburg, J. 1997. *An American Safari: Adventures on the North American Prairie.* New York: Walker.
Cole, N. 1990. *The Final Tide.* New York: McElderry Books.
Edmonds, Y. 1993. *Yuit.* Toronto: Napoleon.
Ferris, J. 1984. *Arctic Explorer: The Story of Matthew Henson.* Minneapolis: Carolrhoda Books.
——. 1994. *A Passion for Danger: Nansen's Arctic Adventure.* New York: Philomel Books.
Hall, D. 1979. *The Ox-Cart Man.* New York: Puffin Books.
Hopkins, D. 1995. *Sweet Clara and the Freedom Quilt.* New York: Random House.
Joosse, B. M. 1991. *Mama, Do You Love Me?* San Francisco: Chronicle Books.
Kellogg, S. 1996. *Johnny Appleseed.* New York: William Morrow.
Kendall, R. 1992. *Eskimo Boy: Life in an Inupiaq Eskimo Village.* New York: Scholastic.
Kinsey-Warnock, N. 1996. *The Fiddler of the Northern Lights.* New York: Cobblehill Books.
Lerner, C. *The Backyard Birds of Summer.* New York: Morrow Junior Books.
MacLachlan, P. 1985. *Sarah, Plain and Tall.* New York: Harper and Row Junior Books.
Newman, S. P. 1983. *The Inuits.* New York: Franklin Watts.
Pearson, K. 1989. *The Sky Is Falling.* Toronto: Puffin Books.
Sandler, M. W. 1995. *Immigrants.* New York: HarperCollins.
Spier, P. 1990. *The Erie Canal.* New York: Doubleday.
Yolen, J. 1996. *Welcome to the Sea of Sand.* New York: G. P. Putnam's Sons.

Middle American Realm

Agard, J. 1989. *The Calypso Alphabet*. New York: Henry Holt.

Argueta, M. 1990. *Magic Dogs of the Volcanoes*. San Francisco: Children's Book Press.

Ashabranner, B. 1987. *The Vanishing Border*. New York: Dodd, Mead.

Bryan, A. 1987. *The Dancing Granny*. New York: Simon and Schuster Children's Books.

——. 1993. *Turtle Knows Your Name*. New York: Simon and Schuster Children's Books.

Ciavonne, J. 1995. *Carlos, Light the Farolito*. New York: Clarion Books.

D'aulaire, I., and E. P. D'aulaire. 1992. *Columbus*. New York: Bantam Doubleday Dell Books for Young Readers.

Ehlert, L. 1996. *Cuckoo: A Mexican Folktale*. New York: Harcourt Brace.

Fisher, L. 1988. *Pyramid of the Sun, Pyramid of the Moon*. New York: Macmillan.

Fritz, J. 1992. *The Great Adventure of Christopher Columbus*. New York: The Putnam Publishing Group.

Gollub, M. 1994. *The Moon Was at a Fiesta*. New York: Tambourine Books.

Griffin, A. 1996. *Rainy Season*. Boston: Houghton Mifflin Children's Books.

Hubley, J., and P. Hubley. 1985. *A Family in Jamaica*. Minneapolis: Lerner Publications.

Lasky, K. 1994. *Days of the Dead*. New York: Hyperion Books for Children.

Lattimore, D. N. 1987. *The Flame of Peace: A Tale of the Aztecs*. New York: Harper and Row.

Lessac, F. 1994. *Caribbean Alphabet*. New York: HarperCollins.

——. 1994. *Caribbean Canvas*. Honesdale, PA: Boyd Mills Press.

Mike, J. M. 1993. *Opossum and the Great Firemaker*. Mahwah, NJ: Troll Associates.

O'Dell, S. 1990. *My Name Is Not Angelica*. New York: Houghton Mifflin.

Parker, N. W. 1996. *Locks, Crocs, and Skeeters*. New York: Greenwillow.

Presilla, M. E. 1994. *Feliz Noche Buena, Feliz Navidad: Christmas Feasts of the Hispanic Caribbean*. New York: Henry Holt.

Pomerantz, C. 1989. *The Chalk Doll*. New York: Lippincott.

Riecken, N. 1996. *Today Is the Day*. Boston: Houghton Mifflin Children's Books.

Staub, F. 1996. *Children of the Yucatan*. Minneapolis: Carolrhoda Books.

Winter, J. 1991. *Diego*. New York: Alfred A. Knopf.

Wisniewski, D. 1991. *The Rain Player*. New York: Clarion Books.

Wolkstein, D. 1981. *The Banza*. New York: Dial Books for Young Readers.

——. 1978. *The Magic Orange Tree, and Other Haitian Folk Tales*. New York: Alfred A. Knopf.

Wood, T. 1992. *The Aztecs*. New York: Viking.

South American Realm

Brusca, M. C. 1994. *My Mama's Little Ranch on the Pampas*. New York: Henry Holt.

Cherry, L. 1990. *The Great Kapok Tree*. San Diego: Harcourt Brace Jovanovich.

deJenkins, L. B. 1996. *So Loud a Silence*. New York: Lodestar Books.

Dorros, A. 1991. *Tonight Is Carnaval*. New York: Dutton Children's Books.

Ehlert, L. 1992. *Moon Rope: A Peruvian Folktale*. San Diego: Harcourt Brace Jovanovich.

Flora. 1989. *Feathers Like a Rainbow: An Amazon Indian Tale*. New York: HarperCollins Children's Books.

George, J. C. 1990. *One Day in the Tropical Rain Forest*. New York: HarperCollins Children's Books.

Goodman, S. E. 1995. *Bats, Bugs, and Biodiversity: Adventures in the Amazonian Rain Forest*. New York: Atheneum Books for Young Readers.

Jordan, M., and T. Jordan. 1992. *Journey of the Red-Eyed Tree Frog*. New York: Simon and Schuster.

Lessem, D. 1995. *Inside the Amazing Amazon*. New York: Crown Publishers.

Lourie, P. 1991. *Amazon: A Young Reader's Look at the Last Frontier*. Honesdale, PA: Caroline House.

Palacios, A. 1993. *The Llama's Secret*. Mahwah, NJ: Troll Associates.

St. John, J. 1986. *A Family in Bolivia*. Minneapolis: Lerner Publications.

North African/Southwest Asian Realm

Abodaher, D. J. 1990. *Youth in the Middle East: Voices of Despair*. New York: Franklin Watts.

Bradford, K. 1996. *There Will Be Wolves*. New York: Lodestar Books.

Climo, S. 1989. *The Egyptian Cinderella*. New York: HarperCollins.

dePaola, T. 1996. *Bill and Pete Go Down the Nile*. New York: The Putnam and Grosset Group.

Dolphin, L. 1993. *Neve Shalom Wahat al-Salaam: Oasis of Peace*. New York: Scholastic.

Edwards, M. 1994. *Chicken Man*. New York: Lothrop, Lee and Shepard Books.

Feder, H. K. 1995. *The Mystery of the Kaifeng Scroll*. Minneapolis: Lerner Publications.

Goldsmith, L. 1993. *The Children of Mauritania: Days in the Desert and by the River Shore*. Minneapolis: Carolrhoda Books.

Heide, F. P., and J. H. Gilliland. 1990. *The Day of Ahmed's Secret*. New York: Lothrop, Lee and Shepard Books.

Kiesler, K. 1996. *Temple Cat*. New York: Clarion Books.

London, J. 1997. *Ali, Child of the Desert*. New York: Lothrop, Lee and Shepard Books.

Moerbeek, K., and C. Dijs. 1988. *Six Brave Explorers*. Los Angeles: Price/Stern/Sloan.

Waldman, N. *The Never-Ending Greenness*. New York: Morrow Junior Books.

Subsaharan African Realm

Angelou, M. 1994. *My Painted House, My Friendly Chicken, and Me*. New York: Clarkson Potter.

Barboza, S. 1994. *Door of No Return: The Legend of Goree Island*. New York: Cobblehill Books.

Brown, M. 1982. *Shadow*. New York: Aladdin Books.

Cowen-Fletcher, J. 1994. *It Takes a Village*. New York: Scholastic.

Farmer, N. 1996. *The Warm Place*. New York: Puffin Books.

Feelings, M. 1985. *Jambo Means Hello: Swahili Alphabet Book*. New York: Dial Books for Children.

Geraghty, P. 1994. *The Hunter*. New York: Crown.

Gordon, S. 1987. *Waiting for the Rain*. New York: Orchard Books.

Grifalconi, A. 1986. *The Village of Round and Square Houses*. Boston: Little, Brown.

Haskins, J. 1989. *Count Your Way Through Africa*. Minneapolis: Carolrhoda Books.

Kreikemeier, G. S. 1993. *Come with Me to Africa: A Photographic Journey*. New York: Golden Press.

Kroll, V. 1995. *Jaha and Jamil Went Down the Hill*. Watertown, MA: Charlesbridge.

Mann, K. 1996. *African Kingdoms of the Past*. Parsippany, NJ: Dillon Press.

Margolies, B. 1990. *Rehema's Journey*. New York: Scholastic.

Medearis, A. S. 1995. *Too Much Talk*. Cambridge, MA: Candlewick Press.

Mennen, I., and N. Daily. 1992. *Somewhere in Africa*. New York: Dutton Children's Books.

Mollel, T. M. 1993. *The King and the Tortoise*. New York: Clarion Books.

——. 1993. *The Princess Who Lost Her Hair: An Akamba Legend*. Mahwah, NJ: Troll Associates.

Onyefulu, I. 1993. *A Is for Africa*. New York: Cobblehill Books.

——. 1996. *Ogbo: Sharing Life in an African Village*. San Diego: Gulliver Books.

Sisulu, E. B. 1996. *The Day Gogo Went to Vote*. Boston: Little, Brown.
Steptoe, J. 1987. *Mufaro's Beautiful Daughters*. New York: Lothrop, Lee and Shepard Books.
Stewart, D. 1996. *Gift of the Sun*. New York: Farrar, Straus and Giroux.
Stock, C. 1990. *Armien's Fishing Trip*. New York: Morrow Junior Books.
Williams, K. L. 1990. *Galimoto*. New York: Lothrop, Lee and Shepard Books.
——. 1991. *When Africa Was Home*. New York: Orchard Books.
Wisniewski, D. 1992. *Sundiata: Lion King of Mali*. New York: Clarion Books.
Yoshida, T. 1989. *Young Lions*. New York: Philomel Books.

South Asian Realm

Bannerman, H., and F. Marcellanos. 1996. *The Story of Little Babaji*. New York: HarperCollins.
Bash, B. 1996. *In the Heart of the Village*. San Francisco: Sierra Club Books for Children.
Bosse, M. 1995. *Tusk and Stone*. New York: Puffin Books.
Brown, M. 1961. *Once a Mouse …* New York: Aladdin Books.
Demi. 1996. *Buddha*. New York: Henry Holt.
Margolies, B. A. 1992. *Kanu of Kathmandu: A Journey in Nepal*. New York: Four Winds Press.
Martin, R. 1997. *The Monkey Bridge*. New York: Alred A. Knopf.
McKibbon, H. W., and S. Cameron. 1996. *The Token Gift*. Toronto: Annick Press.
Miller, L. 1988. *The Black Hat Dances: Two Buddhist Boys in the Himalayas*. New York: Dodd, Mead.
Newton, P. 1990. *The Stone Cutter*. New York: G. P. Putnam's Sons.
Rose, D. L. 1990. *The People Who Hugged the Trees*. Niwot, CO: Roberts Rinehart.
Severance, J. B. 1997. *Gandhi: Great Soul*. New York: Clarion Books.
Staples, S. F. 1989. *Shabanu: Daughter of the Wind*. New York: Alfred A. Knopf.

East Asian Realm

Baker, K. 1989. *The Magic Fan*. San Diego: Harcourt Brace.
Balgassi, H. 1996. *Peacebound Trains*. New York: Clarion Books.
Brenner, B., and J. Takaya. 1996. *Chibi: A True Story from Japan*. New York: Clarion Books.
Buck, P. A. 1986. *The Big Wave*. New York: HarperCollins Children's Books.
Coatsworth, E. 1990. *The Cat Who Went to Heaven*. New York: Simon and Schuster Children's Books.
Fabian, E. 1993. *Adventure in Splendid China*. San Francisco: Getherease.
Fisher, L. E. 1986. *The Great Wall of China*. New York: Macmillan.
Greene, E. 1996. *Ling-Li and the Phoenix Fairy*. New York: Clarion Books.
Hamanaka, S. 1993. *Screen of Frogs*. New York: Orchard Books.
Han, O. S., and S. H. Plunkett. 1994. *Kongi and Potgi: A Cinderella Story from Korea*. New York: Dial Books for Young Readers.
Irwin, H. 1987. *Kim-Kimi*. New York: Simon and Schuster Children's Books.
Kuroyanagi, T. 1996. *Totto-Chan: The Little Girl at the Window*. London: Kodansha America.
Namioka, L. 1994. *Yang the Youngest and His Terrible Ear*. Boston: Little, Brown.
Reddix, V. 1991. *Dragon Kite of the Autumn Moon*. New York: Lothrop, Lee and Shepard Books.
Reeser, M. 1993. *Huan Ching and the Golden Fish*. Austin, TX: Steck-Vaughn.
Rumford, J. 1996. *The Cloud Makers*. Boston: Houghton Mifflin Children's Books.
San Souci, R. D. 1990. *The Enchanted Tapestry: A Chinese Folktale*. New York: Dial Books for Young Readers.

——. 1992. *The Samurai's Daughter.* New York: Dial Books for Young Readers.

Say, A. 1991. *Tree of Cranes.* Boston: Houghton Mifflin.

——. 1993. *Grandfather's Journey.* Boston: Houghton Mifflin.

——. 1994. *The Ink-Keeper's Apprentice.* Boston: Houghton Mifflin.

Snyder, D. 1988. *The Boy of the Three Year Nap.* Boston: Houghton Mifflin.

Uchida, Y. 1985. *The Happiest Ending.* New York: Simon and Schuster Children's Books.

——. 1985. *Samurai of Gold Hill.* Berkeley, CA: Creative Arts Book.

——. 1992. *Journey Home.* New York: Simon and Schuster Children's Books.

——. 1993. *The Best Bad Thing.* New York: Simon and Schuster Children's Books.

Vagin, V., and F. Asch. 1989. *Here Comes the Cat!* New York: Scholastic.

Wisniewski, D. 1989. *The Warrior and the Wise Man.* New York: Lothrop, Lee and Shepard Books.

Yashima, T. 1983. *Crow Boy.* New York: Puffin Books.

Young, E., trans. 1989. *Lon Po Po: A Red-Riding Hood Story from China.* New York: Philomel Books.

Southeast Asian Realm

Breckler, R. 1996. *Sweet Dried Apples: A Vietnamese Wartime Childhood.* Boston: Houghton Mifflin Children's Books.

Cha, D. 1996. *Dia's Story Cloth.* New York: Lee and Low Books.

Garland, S. 1997. *The Lotus Seed.* San Diego: Harcourt Brace.

Ho, M. 1996. *Hush! A Thai Lullaby.* New York: Orchard Books.

Kinkade, S. 1996. *Children of the Philippines.* Minneapolis: Carolrhoda Books.

Lee, J. M. 1991. *The Silent Lotus.* New York: Farrar, Straus and Giroux.

Wartski, M. 1980. *A Boat to Nowhere.* New York: Penguin Books.

Xiong, B. Adapted by C. Spagnoli. 1989. *Nine-in-One Grr! Grr!* San Francisco: Children's Book Press.

Australian Realm

Blumberg, R. 1991. *The Remarkable Voyages of Captain Cook.* New York: Bradbury Press.

Catling, P. S. 1987. *John Midas in the Dreamtime.* New York: Bantam Books.

Crew, G. 1993. *Angel's Gate.* New York: Simon and Schuster Books for Young Readers.

Fox, M. 1989. *Koala Lou.* San Diego: Harcourt Brace.

Lattimore, D. N. 1993. *Punga, the Goddess of Ugly.* San Diego: Harcourt Brace.

Mahy, M. 1995. *Good Fortunes Gang, No. 1: The Cousins Quartet.* New York: Delacorte Press.

Marshall, J. V. 1984. *Walkabout.* Littletown, MA: Sundance.

Nunukul, O. 1993. *Dreamtime: Aboriginal Stories.* New York: Lothrop, Lee and Shepard Books.

Sheehan, P. 1988. *Kylie's Song.* Santa Barbara, CA: Advocacy Press.

Thiele, C. 1986. *Farmer Schulz's Ducks.* New York: Harper and Row.

Vaughan, M. 1994. *Snap!* New York: Scholastic.

Winch, G. 1990. *Enoch the Emu.* Cairns, Australia: Childset.

Pacific Realm

Blumberg, R. 1991. *The Remarkable Voyages of Captain Cook.* New York: Bradbury Press.

Fradin, D. B. 1994. *From Sea to Shining Sea, Hawaii.* Chicago: Children's Press.

Goforth, S. L. 1993. *Tutu and the Ti Plant*. Honolulu: MnM Publishing.

Kudlinski, K. V. 1993. *Pearl Harbor Is Burning! A Story of World War II*. New York: Puffin Books.

Maness, M. 1993. *The Toad that Taught Flying*. Camuela, HI: Pacific Greetings.

Margolies, B. A. 1993. *Warriors, Wigmen, and the Crocodile People: Journeys in Papua New Guinea*. New York: Four Winds Press.

Watkins, T. H. 1996. "The Greening of the Empire, Sir Joseph Banks." *National Geographic* 190(5):28–53.

The World

Collier, J. 1993. *The Backyard Birds of Summer*. New York: Viking Press.

Durell, A., K. Paterson, and J. C. George, eds. 1993. *The Big Book for Our Planet*. New York: Dutton Children's Books.

Iverson, D. 1993. *I Celebrate Nature*. Nevada City, CA: Dawn Publications.

Lauber, P. 1990. *How We Learn the Earth Is Round*. New York: HarperCollins.

Schmid, E. 1992. *The Air Around Us*. New York: North-South Books.

Schuett, S. 1995. *Somewhere in the World Right Now*. New York: Alfred A. Knopf.

Spier, P. 1993. *Noah's Ark*. Garden City, NY: Doubleday.

Getting Your Bearings

The authors wish to acknowledge the following reference books for information concerning the "Getting Your Bearings" sections for each chapter and the glossary.

Adams, S., A. Ganeri, and A. Kay. 1996. *The DK Geography of the World*. New York: DK Publishing.

Allen, W. L., ed. 1995. *National Geographic Atlas of the World*, 6th ed. revised. Washington, DC: National Geographic Society.

Burton, F. G., and R. Lea. 1996. *World Nature Encyclopedia: Northern Asia*. Milwaukee, WI: Raintree.

Farndon, J. 1994. *Dictionary of the Earth*. New York: DK Publishing.

Liebeck, H., and E. Pollard, eds. 1995. *The Oxford English Minidictionary*, 4th ed. New York: Oxford University Press.

The New Encyclopaedia Britannica, 15th ed., vols. 1–30. 1994. Chicago: Encyclopedia Britannica.

The New Grolier Student Encyclopaedia, vols. 1–10. 1991. Danbury, CT: Grolier Educational Corporation.

The World Book Encyclopedia, vols. A–Z. 1996. Chicago: World Book.

Appendix:
Geography for Life–
National Geography Standards (1994)

Element I: The World in Spatial Terms

Standard 1. How to use maps and other geographic representations, tools, and technologies to acquire, process, and repoert information from a spatial perspective.

Standard 2. How to use mental maps to organize information about people, places, and environments in a spatial context.

Standard 3. How to analyze the spatial organization of people, places, and environments on Earth's surface.

Element II: Places and Regions

Standard 4. The physical and human characteristics of a place.

Standard 5. That people create regions to interpret Earth's complexity.

Standard 6. How culture and experience influence people's perceptions of places and regions.

Element III: Physical Systems

Standard 7. The physical processes that shape the patterns of Earth's surface.

Standard 8. The characteristics and spatial distribution of ecosystems on Earth's surface.

Element IV: Human Systems

Standard 9. The characteristics, distribution, and migration of human population on Earth's surface.

Standard 10. The characteristics, distribution, and complexity of Earth's cultural mosaics.

Standard 11. The patterns and networks of economic interdependence on Earth's surface.

Standard 12. The processes, patterns, and functions of human settlement.

Standard 13. How the forces of cooperation and conflict among people influence the division and control of Earth's surface.

Element V: Environment and Society

Standard 14. How human actions modify the physical environment.

Standard 15. How physical systems affect human systems.

Standard 16. The changes that occur in the meaning, use, distribution, and importance of resources.

Element VI: The Uses of Geography

Standard 17. How to apply geography to interpret the past.

Standard 18. How to apply geography to interpret the present and plan for the future.

Index